Contents

Introduction   v

1 Photography and film   1
2 Water   14
3 Drama   27
4 The beach   41
5 The fairground   54
6 Music   66
7 Light and dark   79
8 Friendship and teamwork   94
9 The media   109
10 Space   122
11 Sport   135
12 Puzzles and problem solving   148
13 The circus   161
14 The rainforest   173
15 Dinosaurs   189

Consultation   203

Appendix: Example advertising programme   208

Index   209

Dedication

For Nick.

With love and thanks to all the fantastic children who passed through the doors of Playtime Out of School Club in Cullompton, Devon.

A Practical Guide to Activities for Older Children

Miranda Walker

Published in 2007 by:
Nelson Thornes Ltd
Delta Place
27 Bath Road
CHELTENHAM
GL53 7TH
United Kingdom

07 08 09 10 11 / 10 9 8 7 6 5 4 3 2 1

A catalogue record for this book is available from the British Library

ISBN 978 0 7487 8128 7

Cover photograph by Jim Wileman
Illustrations by Pantek Arts Ltd
Page make-up by Pantek Arts Ltd, Maidstone, Kent

Printed and bound in Croatia by Zrinski

Photograph credits
With special thanks to all the children at the Playtime Out of School Club for their help with the photos. Mark Passmore/Apex, p. 21; Jim Wileman/Apex, pp. 21 and 175.

Photographer: Jim Wileman, **www.jimwileman.co.uk**

Introduction

This book is a practical guide to planning activities in play settings for children aged 4–16 years. With a clear focus on promoting fun, freedom and flexibility, activities covering a range of referenced aspects of play are grouped into 15 exciting, ready-to-use themes for ages 4–12 years. Extension ideas for older children are included. This book is intended for those working in play settings such as out-of-school clubs, and students undertaking courses including NVQs in Children's Care, Learning and Development, and Playwork.

Children attend play settings in their leisure time, so they should participate in planned activities freely, opting in and out of them as they wish. The term 'planned' isn't intended to mean 'formal', as you'll read below. You should also see the section on Consultation on page 203, which outlines why and how you can involve children in the planning process.

Although this isn't a theoretical book about play, it's strongly recommended that the themes and activities suggested are always provided alongside plenty of unthemed, unplanned free play opportunities. Planned activities shouldn't replace free play, but they can certainly complement it. Themes are a fun, meaningful way to link planned activities. They're also a great way to ring the changes and broaden children's experiences within the play setting.

Focusing on a central topic often inspires creative and unusual activities. For instance, despite arranging out-of-school activities for years, it never occurred to me to set up a coconut shy or run an airbrush art workshop until I planned a fairground theme.

Age ranges

The terms used to refer to children of particular ages can be confusing. To clarify, playwork is carried out with children aged 4½–16 years of age. In this book, the broad terms 'younger children' and 'older children' are used to refer to children within the playwork age range.

The term 'young people' is sometimes used to refer to teenagers. However, it isn't used in this book. This is to avoid making the activities too prescriptive in terms of which children they are suitable for. Some under-13s in your setting are likely to be interested in the same activities as teenagers, for example. It's best to consider the activities and extension ideas in the light of the individual children who attend your group – their interests, levels of development and maturity – and to provide activities accordingly. In short, read the extension ideas and then decide if they're suitable for your setting.

You'll find that most of the themes and many of the activities have wide appeal regardless of age. They will work well simultaneously on different levels, as the children in mixed age settings will interpret the activities in a personal way. Some themes, such as 'Dinosaurs', are likely to have a younger appeal, while the 'Media' theme is more sophisticated.

Features

The following features are included in each chapter.

Theme title

The titles of each theme are self-explanatory, for instance, 'The circus' and 'Photography and film'. Although the activities are grouped in themes, each activity also stands alone, enabling you to dip into the book when planning if you want to adopt a non-themed approach.

Since themes aren't intended to be prescriptive there's no 'right' length of time for each to last – you can tailor them to suit your group. But there's certainly scope for each theme to be offered for up to a week by the typical holiday club.

Aspects of play and SPICE

For many years the term **SPICE** has been used as shorthand to refer to five broad areas of children's development, which are:

S Social development

P Physical development (both fine and gross motor)

I Intellectual development

C Creative development

E Emotional development.

Many play practitioners like to refer to **SPICE** when planning their activity programmes. Checking they've included play activities that promote each area of development helps them to offer a good balance of activities overall. To assist with this, each activity included in the book is linked to **SPICE**. Letters appear in bold print after the title of activities to show which aspects of play and development may be promoted. For example, the letter **S** indicates that the activity includes social aspects.

A Practical Guide to Activities for Older Children

Playwork theorist Fraser Brown is credited with coining the term **SPICE**. In recent years he's explained that he believes the **three Fs – fun, freedom and flexibility** – should also be provided alongside activities that promote **SPICE**.

This book fully embraces the **three Fs**. The spirit of **fun, freedom and flexibility** are at the heart of each of the themes and activities. This is expressed in the 'Aspects of play' feature that appears at the start of each theme.

Resources to support free play

You can provide resources which enable children to explore themes further in their free play, should they wish to. Examples are given for each theme. For instance, during the 'Light and dark' theme you may provide free access to torches.

Activities

Flexibility

Although children should freely choose to participate in planned activities, some play practitioners find it hard to maintain a flexible approach when they've taken the trouble to organise resources and so on. But activities that are interesting, fun and exciting will naturally attract children, and consultation will help you to ensure that you're providing pursuits children want to engage with.

Having said that, sometimes an activity fails to get going, or soon fizzles out, and you have to change tack. It's just something that happens sometimes. On another occasion the group dynamic can be different and the same activity is the hit of the day. Children will sometimes take activities in unexpected directions, or do something different than intended with the resources provided. That's great! They've made the activity their own. Remember that **fun, freedom and flexibility** are the key. Make the **three Fs** your activity mantra!

Mix and match the activities suggested in each theme to suit your group. Don't feel you should always follow the instructions to the letter – borrow from the activities, adapt them as you wish, and use them to complement the group's own ideas. (There's no such thing as an exhaustive list of activities for any theme – they are only ever works in progress.)

Equipment

The equipment needed for each activity is listed. Many resources including paper, card and items such as large cardboard tubes can be found at scrap stores. These stores collect suitable waste materials from industry and businesses, and make them available cheaply to play settings. For instance, camera film canisters discarded by photo-labs can be salvaged and used in craft activities. Call your local authority to locate a scrap store in your area.

Instructions

Each theme features a variety of activities from arts and crafts to games and recipes. It's always advisable to have a trial run at following the instructions for crafts and skills (such as juggling) before embarking on the activities with children. Generally, the activity instructions given are intended for children. When an adult should carry out a task themselves – such as drilling a hole on behalf of younger children – this is indicated separately in the text.

Links

Some activities can be effectively linked with other themes. For instance, during the 'Sport' theme you may like to incorporate some teamwork activities from the 'Friendship and teamwork' theme. These links are specified in the text.

Taglines

Advertising

Once you've selected a theme and activities, you need to let children and their parents know about them.

Many play settings (particularly holiday clubs) advertise their provision locally by publishing their programme of activities in the form of fliers and posters. An example advertising programme is provided in the Appendix on page 208. You'll see that, after the title of each activity listed, an interesting tagline is used to expand a bit more, revealing a flavour of the activity. After each activity within this book, such a tagline appears in handwritten style print. You can use the taglines (or variations on them) in your programmes, enabling you to draw up promotional material quickly and easily after selecting activities to include in your programme.

On the day

You can inform children about the activities available at each session by writing the day's activity titles and taglines on a poster or board displayed near the entrance. This helps to create a buzz about forthcoming activities, which can motivate children to participate.

Good practice

Risk assessment

Because this book is intended for play settings, it's assumed that all activities will take place under the supervision of adults. Close supervision may sometimes be required for some activities. The appropriate level of supervision for your group will largely depend on the age and abilities of the children participating in each activity.

Reminders of good practice are given after some activities within the book. However, you must rely on your own judgement and with regard to your setting's health and safety policy, you should risk assess the activities within the context of your own group. This includes ensuring that:

- equipment is safe, and that it is used safely
- good hygiene procedures are followed (such as washing hands before/ after specific activities, following food preparation regulations, etc.)
- safeguards are in place to protect children from harm when using computers.

Inclusion

It's crucial to good practice to ensure the activities you offer meet the individual needs of the children attending your setting. Consider this when planning your programme, and make any necessary adaptations accordingly.

Healthy eating

Some themes include recipes for healthy snacks. There are also a few additional recipes for foods such as biscuits and cake. These are intended as occasional treats offered as part of a balanced diet.

Competition

Many of the games included can be played competitively or non-competitively, so adapt them to suit your needs. It's a good idea to include a mixture of both types of games in your programme. You may like to offer small prizes from time to time.

Extension ideas

Extension ideas are included after some activities. These generally outline how activities can be adapted or built upon to suit to older children.

Websites

A list of relevant websites is provided at the end of each theme. Some of these sites are intended for play practitioners, and some are suitable for children to access. Do check the tone and content of the children's sites as this changes frequently, such is the nature of the internet. In addition to these websites, you may like to visit **www.mirandawalker.co.uk** for further activity suggestions.

1 Photography and film

Aspects of play

Advancing technology has made a photography and film theme practical for group settings. Digital cameras start at reasonable prices, and some children carry one with them as a feature on their mobile phones. Many groups have access to a computer and so digital photos can be viewed on the screen instantly, without the cost and delay of film development. Video cameras can be hired reasonably for short periods.

Photography and film in many forms can be explored during this theme. You may also like to incorporate some of the activities suggested within the 'Drama' theme (see page 27).

Resources to support free play

- Cameras
- Printing facilities
- Basic photo editing software
- Video camera
- Internet access
- Related non-fiction books
- Magazines
- Pictures

✓ Good practice

Remember to get written permission from parents and carers before children are photographed or filmed. You should explain how the pictures or footage will be used.

Learning to use a camera

"Learn the top five tips for fantastic photos!"

Once children have mastered the basics, teach them the following tips.

- **Flash** Use a flash outdoors, even on a sunny day. It will lighten dark shadows.
- **Vertical pictures** Turn the camera sideways and take vertical pictures too. This is often the best way to take photos of people and statues.
- **Close-ups** Stand in close and fill the frame with the subject.
- **Backgrounds** Choose a plain background that won't detract from the subject. This stops people appearing as though they have things in the background balanced on their heads!
- **Eye level** Get down to the eye level of the subject to really capture their face. This works well with animals as well as people.

Special effects

"Take sensational snaps using special effects."

Equipment
- Camera
- Stocking
- Hairspray

Instructions

To create a soft effect
- Experiment with breathing on the lens before taking a picture.
- Try placing a piece of stocking over the lens and shoot through this.
- Spray some hairspray in the air and shoot through the mist.

To create a motion/speed effect

- With the flash on, spin the camera quickly downwards as you take a picture. This gives a blurred effect, but at the moment the flash fires the subject is stilled.
- As above, but this time quickly pan the camera across as you take the picture.
- Try these techniques when taking pictures of faces to create some weird and wonderful images.

To create silhouettes

Take simple shots against a bright background (a bright sky is ideal, but don't shoot into the sun). Turn the flash off for a bold image.

To create unusual, dramatic perspectives

Experiment with the zoom facility. Try taking the same shot with both wide and longer lenses. Use this technique when shooting subjects that can be recognised easily or the effect of the unusual perspective will be lost.

Editing

With a computer program, the children can edit their pictures. Young children will be able to do tasks such as cropping and improving picture quality, while older children can achieve a range of special effects.

Snap happy!

Extension Idea

For older children, invite a photographer (perhaps from your local newspaper) to demonstrate their skills to the group. Digital cameras allow the children to see the pictures taken immediately. They can find out about the styles of photography used in different media.

Pinhole viewer

"Find out how photography works and make a viewer to take home."

ACTIVITY

Equipment
- Black film canister
- Opaque sticky tape (such as Scotch tape)
- Scissors
- Drawing pin
- A4 sheet black paper

Instructions

This activity demonstrates how photography works.

1. Carefully push a drawing pin in the centre of the bottom of a film canister, in order to poke a small hole (or 'aperture' in photography terms).

2. To create a viewing screen, cover the opening of the canister by stretching opaque sticky tape across and sticking it down. You will need to use two pieces side by side.

3. Place the canister on the paper as shown in the diagram on the page opposite. Roll the paper into a tube around the canister so that no light can come in. Secure with a piece of sticky tape.

4. Use the pinhole viewer in a well-lit area. Look through the paper tube, and point the viewer at an object. You will see an upside-down image of the object projected onto the screen. (The flipped image is due to light travelling in a straight line through a small aperture.)

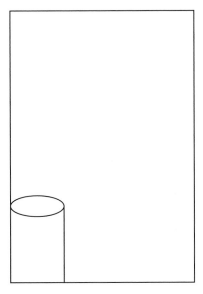

Line up the viewing screen end of the canister
with the edge of the paper

Pinhole viewer

ACTIVITY

Cartridge cameras

❝Make your own working pinhole camera.❞

Equipment
- 126 cartridge camera film
- Black paper
- Thin black card
- Thick black card

▶

- Scissors
- Ruler
- Pencil
- Craft knife
- Aluminium foil
- 2 strong rubber bands
- No. 10 sewing needle
- Black insulation tape
- Coin

Instructions

This activity is best suited to older children. Precise measuring is important.

1. Make a box (which will form the back of the camera) with thin card. Cut the card into a strip measuring 133 mm × 280 mm. With a ruler and pencil, divide the strip into four equal squares.
2. Score the pencil lines with a craft knife. Fold into a box shape and tape along the whole length of each edge with the insulation tape.
3. Cut a 25 mm square of aluminium foil. Gently make a very tiny hole in the centre with the tip of the needle.
4. Cut a piece of thick (rigid) card measuring 38 mm × 70 mm. Cut a 13 mm square opening in the centre with the craft knife.
5. Put the foil square over this opening. Take care to ensure the tiny hole is central.
6. Use insulation tape to secure on all four sides so no light will enter.
7. To make the front of the camera, cut a 25 mm square from the paper. Place it precisely over the foil. Tape down securely on the top edge. This is the shutter. Use a tiny piece of tape to temporarily secure the bottom edge (this will be removed to take pictures).
8. Fit the thin card box behind the front of the camera. Eliminate light by taping generously on all sides.
9. You must use a 126 cartridge film (such as Kodak Gold 200). You'll see the film has a grooved recess in a square opening. The back of the camera will fit into the film cartridge. Don't worry that it's a tight fit – this eliminates light.
10. To keep the camera holding together firmly, use a rubber band on each end.
11. There is a round opening on the top of the film cartridge. Insert a coin and turn slowly to wind on the film. Watch the film indicator to see when the film is in picture-taking position.

Taking pictures with your camera

1. Take photos outside in daylight. There is no viewfinder, so pictures are lined up by looking over the camera. Place the camera on a solid surface such as a table, taping it in place if necessary (i.e. if there's a breeze).

2. Open the shutter by removing the tiny piece of tape and pushing up the flap. Replace the shutter after taking a picture. The time the shutter is open is known as the exposure time. Working out the exposure time isn't an exact science. With Kodak Gold 200 film, try leaving the shutter open for 1.5 seconds in the brightest sunshine and up to 7 seconds in cloudy conditions.

3. You can create different effects by taking three shots of the same subject with varying exposure times.

4. After each picture, wind the film on with the coin.

5. Detach the camera and get the finished film developed at the photo-lab as usual.

Sun photo art

ACTIVITY

SPICE

"Use special paper to take pictures without a camera."

Equipment

- Sun-Print paper, a photographic paper designed for children that makes it possible to make an amazing white-on-blue print in minutes. An internet search will provide you with details of Sun-Print stockists.

Instructions

Place objects of interesting shapes or textures on the photosensitive paper, then leave in the sun. After a few minutes, the image will be printed onto the paper. The children then develop the image in tap water. Objects of an interesting shape or texture such as leaves, flowers or shells make dramatic prints.

Intangible object collections

"Start your own weird and wonderful collections using your camera."

Equipment
- Cameras

Preferably all children will have individual access to a camera during their own time for this on-going activity. A disposable camera would suffice.

Instructions

1. Children love to collect all manner of tangible things, from trading cards to novelty erasers. Engage the group in a discussion about their collections.

2. Ask the children to think about how they could 'collect' through photography things that are intangible, abstract or otherwise difficult to physically collect. For instance, the children could collect snowmen by taking pictures of the ones they see over time. They could collect muddy puddles, bridges, cats or funny signs.

3. Ask the children to start collecting images over the next two or three weeks.

4. Ask the children to bring in their photo collections on a pre-arranged date. Provide resources to enable them to mount and display their collections.

5. The children can continue adding to their collections long after the theme is over.

In the picture

"Get posing for our fast-paced photo game!"

Equipment
- Camera

Instructions

1. When the game is first introduced, appoint an adult to play the role of photographer.

2. The rest of the players should move around the play space in a manner selected by the photographer. For instance, they may be asked to move like an elephant, or to act as though they've just won a talent show, or as if they're looking everywhere for one missing shoe.

3. After the group has milled around using all the space available for a minute or so, the photographer should shout out the name of one of the players. This child must freeze where they are. They will be in the centre of a photograph.

4. The photographer trains the camera on the child and immediately starts to countdown aloud from ten to zero.

5. This is the signal for the other players to quickly gather around the child, arranging themselves in a pose, some standing behind or beside the child, some crouching in front, etc. The aim of the game is to be in the picture, but the children must be quick.

6. The photographer takes the photo as they reach zero in the countdown.

7. The game continues as before. The photographer gives a new style in which players should move around. But this time the countdown goes from eight to zero, so players have to move even faster. Continue to shave 2 seconds off the time in each round, until there are just 2 seconds left. Obviously not all the children will manage to be in all the photos!

8. The end result is an early shot or two of a fairly traditional group pose, leading to some fantastically chaotic snaps of posing players attempting to slide into view! Game photos look great displayed together.

Photo figures

"You'll seem as tiny as a toy in these fun photos!"

ACTIVITY

SPICE

Equipment
- Digital camera and printing facility
- Play figures
- Scissors
- Coloured card
- Dressing up clothes
- Felt-tip pens
- Glue stick

Instructions

1. Demonstrate to the children how taking close-up photos of play figures (people and animals) can make them appear life-size. Print a couple of examples, and cut out the figures.
2. Place these on a sheet of coloured card, which will act as a background. Show the children how a scene could be built up.
3. Take a photo of a child, zooming out to get their whole body in. Print and cut out the body.
4. Compare the two cut-outs, explaining to children that they can play with scale in their photography to make their own bodies and the toy figures appear similar in size. The children can create fun scenarios in this way, especially if they take some snaps of each other in dressing-up outfits.
5. Let the children snap away, experimenting with the technique. There will be some trial and error.
6. The children can play with the cut-outs or paste them onto the card to create a permanent scene.

Link

The photo cut-out figures can be used in conjunction with a puppet theatre. See page 38.

ACTIVITY

Using a video camera

"Use a video camera to make your own film."

Once they have been shown the basics of how to operate a video camera, it's a good idea to allow the children plenty of practice. It's tricky to get the hang of holding the camera steady whilst moving around or zooming. When they're ready, the children can try out their skills in the following activities.

Making an introduction-to-the-setting film, to be shown to new members
This can feature a tour and a montage of activities taking place, complete with commentary.

Vox-pox interviews
Peers are interviewed on camera about a particular subject. This is a great way to consult with the children for evaluation or planning purposes.

Link

Recording drama or replicated factual TV programmes such as the news. See pages 35–7 and 113–114 for further details.

SPICE

Roll the credits

"*Help design end credits and make them roll!*"

Equipment
- Video camera
- Tri-pod (optional)
- Roll of wallpaper
- Felt-tip pens
- Chair

Instructions

The purpose of this activity is to add end credits to a video recording.

1. Cue the video to the end of filming.
2. Unroll the wallpaper.
3. Leave the first 2 m of the wallpaper blank. Thereafter, the children involved in filming each write their name decoratively on the paper with felt-tips, one name under the other.
4. Roll the paper back up.
5. Have one child stand on a chair, holding the roll of paper at either end. A second child should crouch on the ground, facing the chair. Unroll the beginning of the paper (which is blank), and pass it to the crouching child. They should take up the slack.

Allow plenty of filming practice ▶

6. A third child should focus the video camera on the paper, at the midway point between the standing and crouching child. It's their job to operate the camera and hold it steady (you could use a tripod).

7. With the camera recording, the crouching child should gently pull the paper to make it unroll slowly from the hands of their partner, giving the impression of rolling credits.

8. The camera operator should fade out after the last name appears.

Extension Idea

Film making for older children can be a more sophisticated affair. For some it will be an interesting medium to explore temporarily, while for others it may prove to be a precursor to a career in the arts. It's a good idea to enlist the assistance of someone with previous film experience when working on a media theme with the older age range. To find out about current projects taking place in your area, make contact with your regional branch of the Arts Council. (See the website section on page 13.) The Council can also provide you with information about grants for the arts. You may be able to access funds to purchase equipment or to pay for a professional to run a film workshop at your setting.

The youth-work organisation, UK Youth, have set up Film for Youth which features an annual film making festival. Young people interested in film making are encouraged to submit short films of 3–6 minutes to the organisation. These can take the form of a drama, documentary, comedy or animation. There is a lower age category for young people aged 12–15 years. Submissions can be made by individuals or by those working in small groups of five. This makes working on a Film for Youth project ideal for group settings.

Film for Youth sends out a free DVD to those who express interest in the festival. Made especially by Guy Ritchie, it offers help and advice on film making and how to get started. The DVD and additional support is provided through the Film for Youth website (see page 13). Some of the films submitted to Film for Youth are showcased on the website, and some are screened at film festivals around the country.

Why not arrange a special event at the end of this theme to celebrate children's work? Mount children's photographs on the walls (a black background sets off pictures well), and arrange to show the films in an area where you can dim the lights. You may also like to produce a souvenir guide to the exhibition, which includes all the children's names. Lastly, invite children's families and friends along.

Websites

Visit:

www.kodak.com select 'consumer photography' from the menu for tips, tutorials and 'ideas for the classroom' some of which can be adapted to the play setting

www.kodak.com/global/en/consumer/education/lessonPlans/pinholeCamera/ and www.pinholephotography.com.au/ for instructions to make various pinhole cameras, a guide to taking pinhole photos and a gallery of pinhole photography

www.filmforyouth.org/about.htm the site of Film for Youth, with advice for young filmmakers

www.artscouncil.org.uk/index.php for sources of funding for film projects

2 Water

Aspects of play

Many of the same water activities tend to appeal as much to older children as they do to younger ones. You may like to group the outdoor games together in your activity programme and run a one-day 'Water Gala' which could become an eagerly anticipated annual event at your setting.

While most children are happy to get soaked during games, there may be one or two who don't want to get wet. Respect their wishes, and ensure the other children do too. Provide access to plenty of quieter activities such as free play with water trays and traditional water toys alongside the 'getting wet games'.

Ask the children to wear sensible shoes such as trainers when playing water games. A change of dry clothes and a towel will be needed by adults as well as the children. Give some thought to the facilities you can provide to manage the changing of clothes appropriately.

Ensure wet children don't get too cold, and that everyone wears waterproof sun protection if necessary. To avoid slips, be prepared to move around the playground during activities as the floor becomes wet. Wipe up indoor spills as soon as they occur.

Resources to support free play

- Water trays
- Continual access to water supply outside perhaps via a hose
- Water toys such as waterwheels, beakers, jugs, funnels, buckets, water sprayers, etc.

✓ Good practice

Children can drown in just a few centimetres of water, and so it's important to ensure that children are consistently supervised when playing with or near water.

Bulls-eye

ACTIVITY

SPICE

"Hit the bulls-eye to make a splash in our fun target game!"

Equipment
- Large bucket of water
- Soft sponge tennis balls
- Chalk

Instructions

1. Show the children how to draw a large target on the playground floor or an outside wall (see diagram below). Allocate points to each ring of the target, giving the highest number to the bulls-eye.

2. Mark a chalk line on the ground 2 or 3 m away which players must stand behind when taking aim at the target.

3. Place the bucket of water behind the line, and fill it with the soft tennis balls. For a satisfying splash against the target, the children should ensure the balls are completely soaked with water before taking aim!

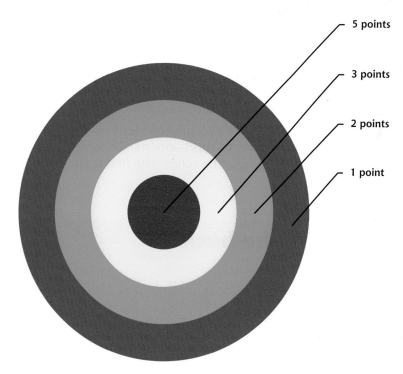

5 points

3 points

2 points

1 point

Bulls-eye target

Under and over

ACTIVITY

SP**I**CE

"*Can your team pass water over and under without getting soaked?*"

Equipment
- Large bucket of water
- Jug
- Large paper cups, one per team

Instructions

In this version of the traditional party game, the usual balloon is replaced by a paper cup filled with water.

1. Split the group into small teams. Five or six per team is ideal.
2. The children line up one behind the other in their teams. They must not turn around for the duration of the game.
3. Fill cups with water to the ¾ mark, and give one cup to the child at the front of each team. He or she will be the team captain.
4. On your signal the game starts. The team leader passes their cup over their head to the player behind them. That player takes the cup and passes it between their legs to the next player. The cup should be passed over and under until it reaches the child at the back. He or she must take the cup and run to the front of the team. They must pass the cup over their head to the next player. Getting wet is part of the fun, but children must try not to spill water as this will slow them down – adults must refill cups as necessary using jugs of water (filled from the bucket).
5. The game continues in the same way until the team captain is back at the front of their team. As soon as this happens, the whole team must quickly sit down, still one behind the other. The first team seated wins the game.

Pass the buck

ACTIVITY

SP**I**CE

"*Pass the buck quickly or you could get wet . . .*"

Equipment
- Balloons
- Access to a tap
- Sticky tape
- Scissors
- Pin

Instructions

1. Fill a few balloons from the tap with as much water as you dare. Tie securely.

2. Cut some short lengths of sticky tape and stick them in random spots around the balloons.

3. It's now possible to pierce holes in the balloons with a pin without bursting them – simply pierce a hole through the pieces of tape. Each balloon is now known as a 'buck'.

4. The children stand in a circle and pass a buck around from one player to the next. As they handle the buck, the pressure will cause the balloon to leak.

5. As the buck becomes slippery, passing it becomes trickier. A player is out if they drop the buck, if the water runs out while they are holding it or if the balloon gives out and bursts on them, soaking them in the process! A new buck should then be introduced to the game.

Extension Idea

When playing with older children you may like to have several bucks being passed around the group at once to speed up the game and increase the risk of getting wet.

ACTIVITY

Balloon volleyball

"Surprise is the name of this game – both hits and misses can make you wet!"

S P I C E

Equipment
- Water filled balloons
- Net

Instructions

Divide the group into two teams and play volleyball as usual with one exception – replace the ball with a water-filled balloon. These are unpredictable to play with, which adds to the fun. You never can tell if they'll burst when a player hits them, or when they land on the floor. Have spare balloons ready and introduce one quickly each time the balloon in play bursts. Be careful not to overfill the balloons or they'll burst too frequently.

Towel lacrosse

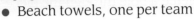

"Put your throwing and catching skills to the test in our fun challenge."

S P I C E

Equipment
- Beach towels, one per team
- Water-filled balloons

Instructions

1. Divide the children into teams of four, and equip each team with a beach towel.
2. Have each child hold onto a corner of their team's towel.
3. Place a water-filled balloon in the centre of each team's towel. On your signal the teams should attempt to toss their balloon in the air and catch it on the towel. The team with the most tosses landed before their balloon bursts wins. If a balloon lands on the floor but does not break it can be retrieved and play can be continued, but the toss will not have earned a point – only tosses landed safely in the towel can be counted.

Extension Idea

Once they've mastered tossing the balloon, older children can try the following:

1. Each team of four joins up with another team. The two teams stand a couple of metres apart.
2. A water-filled balloon is placed in the towel of one team. The children must toss the balloon towards the other team, who must try to catch it in their towel, and then fling it back. Teamwork is required to manoeuvre into position. Once teams can successfully achieve a short rally, they can make the task harder by taking a step or two away from one another.

Skipping challenge

" Can you hold a cup of water while
you skip without getting drenched? **"**

Equipment
- Skipping rope
- Bucket of water
- Paper cup

Instructions

1. Two children should twirl a skipping rope, while the rest of the players line up nearby, next to a bucket of water.

2. Give the first player a paper cup, which they should half fill with water from the bucket. Then, holding the cup, they should attempt to do three skips without spilling the water.

3. After their turn the child should pass the cup to the next player and rejoin the end of the queue if they'd like another go. Remember to alternate the rope twirlers so everyone can have a turn.

Extension Idea

Older children can attempt the task whilst double-dutch skipping (when two ropes are twirled in opposite directions simultaneously).

✔ Good practice

It's particularly important to keep moving position to prevent children from slipping on wet ground during this activity.

Relays

"Can your team save water to win our relay races?**"**

Equipment
- Large buckets of water
- Empty buckets
- Large paper cups
- Skewers/knitting needle
- Sponges
- Chalk
- Hoops, balls, hurdles, etc. (see below)

Instructions

Sponge relay

1. Divide the children into teams and have each team line up at one end of the playground. Put a full bucket of water next to the child at the front of each team. Place a sponge in each bucket.

2. At the other end of the playground place an empty bucket opposite each team.

3. On your signal, the child at the front of each team should soak their sponge in water. Then they run across the playground and wring as much water as possible out of the sponge into their empty bucket. They run back and hand the sponge to the next player on their team, who follows suit.

4. When everyone has had a turn, the team with the most water in their bucket wins the game.

Cup relay

This game is similar to the sponge relay, but a paper cup is used by each team to transport the water rather than a sponge. To make it more interesting, use a skewer to make three holes in the bottom of each cup. The children will need to move across the playground as carefully as possible so not to spill water out of the top of the cup, whilst going as fast as they can to avoid losing all the water out of the bottom.

Obstacle relay

In traditional obstacle races, children are required to take turns travelling across the playground completing a number of tasks along the way, such as scrambling through hoops or stepping over hurdles. When they reach the end of the course the player runs back to tag a team-mate. This continues until everyone has had a turn. This version is played in the same way, but each player must carry a cup of water with them and attempt not to spill it en route. They must pour their remaining water into their empty bucket before running back to tag their team-mate.

Extension Idea

In each of the relays the team with the most water in their bucket wins. However, when playing with older children you may like to build the competition by treating each relay as a separate round of the same game, only measuring which team has the most water at the end of all the relays.

Splash and dash!

Ice bowls

"Make a beautiful, elegant ice bowl complete with frozen decorations.**"**

ACTIVITY

SPICE

Equipment
- Plastic bowls (see below)
- Cooking oil
- Pastry brush
- Edible decorations
- Jug of water
- Access to a freezer

Instructions

1. Each child will need two bowls of different sizes for this activity. One must fit inside the other with 2–3 cm to spare all the way around. Plastic pudding basins are ideal. (You may be able to borrow these in quantity from your local school.) The children should use the pastry brush to lightly grease the outside of the small basin and the inside of the larger basin with the oil.

2. Put the small basin in the middle of larger one, and half fill it with water to weigh it down.

3. Place attractive, edible, decorative items such as blueberries, herb leaves and cake decorations in between the two bowls.

4. Pour water into the space between the bowls (onto the decorations), and place the whole thing in the freezer. Remember to record which child made each bowl.

5. * Once completely set (it's best to leave the bowls overnight), remove from the freezer and stand the whole thing in a sink of lukewarm water for exactly 1 minute.

6. * It should now be possible to carefully ease the inner bowl out (the ice inside is no longer needed). The outside bowl can now be carefully turned out to reveal the elegant ice bowl.

7. You may like to take photos of the children with their frosty creations, so they can look at them long after the ice has turned back to water.

* Younger children will need help with steps 5 and 6.

≫
Link You may like to give the children the opportunity to eat from their ice bowls. Homemade ice cream is the perfect dish to serve. See page 44 for the recipe.

Ice sculptures

"Chill out with this cool activity!"

Equipment

- Water
- Assortment of containers (see below)
- Food colourings
- Access to a freezer
- Paint brushes
- Gloves

Instructions

1. In preparation, fill many containers of various shapes and sizes with water and freeze them until solid. Large blocks of ice can be made by using empty ice-cream containers. Yoghurt pots are also useful, and balloons can be used to make interesting random shapes. Traditional ice cubes are always popular and these days there are also novelty ice moulds available. Interesting smaller shapes can also be made by using plastic trays from chocolate boxes. Colouring some of the water with food colouring adds interest, but use just a little to prevent staining during play.

2. Make sure that the children bring in gloves to protect their hands from the cold and to prevent them becoming stuck to their sculpture!

3. The children sculpt by choosing blocks of ice that appeal to them, and fusing them together to make whatever they feel inspired to – an igloo or a castle, or perhaps a figure or an abstract. Some children may like to collaborate, while others may prefer to work alone. Sometimes blocks will bond when simply held together for a few seconds. However, brushing a little water on each surface beforehand will act as 'glue'.

4. The activity is enhanced by making a range of craft resources available to be added to the sculptures – pipe cleaners, sprinkles and so on. When sculpting outside, the children can be encouraged to incorporate natural materials they find such as twigs and stones, but if you are limited to inside these can always be provided.

5. You may like to take photos of the creations before they melt.

Giant bubbles

*"*Blow gigantic bubbles as big as you can with our special solution and wonderful wands.*"*

To make the solution

Equipment
- 12 cups of water
- 7 tablespoons of glycerine
- 1¼ cups of washing-up liquid
- Clean bucket
- Wooden spoon

Instructions

1. The children should wash a bucket spotlessly clean. Pour in the water and washing-up liquid. A good quality brand gives the best results. Add the glycerine (available from specialist cook shops). This is the secret ingredient that makes the solution strong enough to blow giant bubbles. Adjust the quantities of the recipe to suit your requirements.

2. Blend together by stirring slowly with a wooden spoon so that the solution doesn't foam up. If it does foam, set it aside for a few minutes until settled.

3. Pour the mixture slowly into another vessel for play (such as a water tray). This must be big enough for dipping the wands.

To make giant bubble wands

Equipment
- 50 cm lengths of dowel/garden cane
- Wide nylon cord or thin polypropylene rope
- Scissors

Instructions

1. The lengths of dowel or garden cane should be approximately 50 cm long. If they've been cut to size, sand the ends with sandpaper to avoid splinters.

2. Cut either wide nylon cord (available by the metre from textile shops) or thin polypropylene rope (by the metre from hardware stores) into 60 cm lengths. Narrow nylon cord is unsuitable as it's too lightweight.

3. The children tie one end of their cord/rope around the top of their stick, and tie the other end three quarters of the way down to form a loop.

4. The wands can now be dipped in the bubble solution. Waving the wand gently in the air produces impressive free-form bubbles. Tubular bubbles can be made by holding the wand up, then dropping the arm down.

5. Experiment with the size and shape of bubbles by sliding the knotted ends of their cord/rope up and down the stick.

You may also like to introduce a purchased 'bubble machine' which will turn out strings of small bubbles when filled with solution. Adding a few drops of powder paint or food colouring to the solution will create coloured bubbles. Younger children enjoy chasing these with pieces of paper, catching them to make bubble prints to take home.

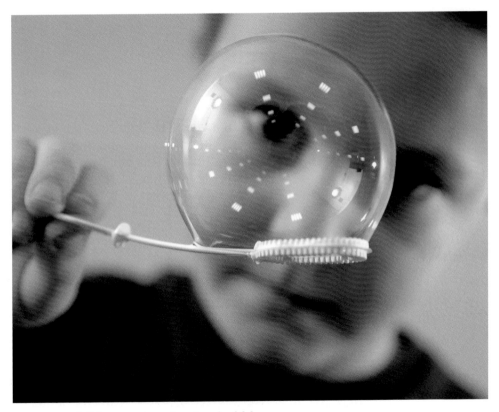

Younger children enjoy chasing bubbles

Spray paint

"Spray your own airbrush-effect art.**"**

Equipment
- Water sprayers
- Water
- Powder paint
- Paper

Instructions

1. Fill the sprayers with water and add a little powder paint to each. Shake to make a watery paint solution.
2. Put sheets of paper on the floor.
3. The children can now create their own airbrush-effect art.

Extension Idea

Provide older children with a giant sized piece of paper and a stronger solution of water and paint and they can collaborate on a piece of graffiti art. This will be valued since the graffiti is in an appropriate place. Don't make the paint too strong or the nozzle will clog.

Websites

Visit:

> **www.123child.com/summer/water.html** for science-related water experiments and creative ideas

> **www.pastor2youth.com/index.php** for water games, select 'games' from the site menu

> **www.nationalgeographic.com/ngkids/trythis/trythis_water_splash.html** for outdoor water games designed for children's parties

3 Drama

Aspects of play

Some people worry about drama as a theme because they've never done any acting themselves. But there's really no need.

We watch TV and films because we like the dramatisation of stories. Most of us are very familiar with the way in which plots unfold, feelings are shown and dialogue is delivered, even if we've never thought much about it. Dramatisation is part of our everyday lives, and you don't have to have drama training to facilitate it.

Children are driven to dramatise in their free play from the time they're very young. Fantasy games and imaginative play grow more sophisticated over time. Children may act out real-life events or create fantastical adventures with complicated plots.

Some children may be reluctant to join in drama activities. Offer encouragement where appropriate, but never pressure children to participate. Ensure you offer plenty of 'behind the scenes' jobs and free-play opportunities. Children take an emotional risk when they perform, so create a culture of receiving performances positively within the group.

Resources to support free play

- Imaginary area/stage
- Dressing up clothes/costumes
- Masks
- Face paints/make-up
- Puppets
- Scripts
- Note-pads and pens
- Video camera
- Tape recording equipment
- Internet access

Children often feel self-conscious at the beginning of drama activities, so it's a good idea to begin with a game that involves a bit of drama and breaks the ice. Several are suggested below. You can wind down sessions in the same way.

ACTIVITY

Mime name game

❝Can you mime your own name?**❞**

Instructions

1. Everyone sits in a circle.

2. Ask the children to think of an adjective or verb that starts with the same letter as their first name. For the purpose of the game, the descriptive word becomes the child's first name, and their first name becomes their second name. For instance, a child may call himself Laughing Liam.

3. Each child must think of a mime or action they can do that will represent their new name, e.g. Laughing Liam may mime doing a big belly laugh.

4. When everyone has decided on a name, one child should be selected to introduce themselves to the group – 'I'm Laughing Liam.' They should then do their mime.

5. The next player must repeat the previous player's name and mime, and then introduce themselves and do their own mime – 'That's Laughing Liam [mime the belly laugh] and I'm Magical Melanie [mime waving a wand].'

6. The third player has to remember two names and mimes before introducing themselves. Continue in the same way around the circle.

7. If a child becomes stuck when trying to recall a name, the relevant mime should be given as a clue.

Improvise!

"Put your improvisational skills to the test!"

Equipment
- Props (see below)

ACTIVITY

S P I C E

Instructions

1. Everyone stands in a circle. Place a number of props in the centre.
2. The first player chooses a prop and does a mime with it. The group must guess what the player is pretending the prop is – the trick is to choose inanimate objects that can be used in several different ways. For instance, a long cardboard tube may be used as a flute, a golf club, etc.
3. Once the mime is guessed, the prop is passed to the next child. When inspiration runs out, introduce a new prop.

White lies

"Little white lies are allowed in this game!"

ACTIVITY

S P I C E

Instructions

1. Everyone stands a circle. The first player should mime doing something recognisable, such as brushing their teeth.
2. The rest of the group call out, 'What are you doing?'
3. The player must now lie. For instance, he or she may say, 'I'm walking my dog!' The lies will usually prompt laughter.
4. Continue clockwise around the circle until everyone has had a turn.

Extension Idea

Older children can play a different version of the game. Steps 1–3 are the same as before. But instead of the second player making up their own mime, they must mime the lie told by the previous player. In our example the player would have to mime walking the dog. The third player will have to mime the second player's lie, and so on.

Link For further drama games which double as ice-breakers, see 'Shark attack' (page 44), 'In the picture' (page 8) and 'The chocolate race' (page 98). Traditional charades also works well.

Dramatic expression with puppets

Powder and paint

"Be a make-up artist and try out the powder and paint!"

Equipment
- Face paints/stage make-up
- Base
- Mirror
- Make-up remover

Instructions

This activity can be done just for fun, or the children may use it to develop a character they will play in performance.

1. Ask the children to find a partner.

2. Depending on the age of the children, make face paints or stage make-up available and follow the instructions regarding their application. For instance, it's advisable to use a baby lotion 'base' with most face paints to make them easier to remove.

3. Give the children the opportunity to paint one another's faces, and then view themselves in the mirror.

Link Also see 'Making masks' on page 85.

✔ Good practice

Obtain parental permission for this activity, and check children do not have allergies which could be triggered by the resources.

Extension Idea

For older children, invite someone from your local theatre or amateur dramatic society to visit the group and demonstrate techniques for applying stage make-up. Learning how to make fake wounds is often popular!

Scriptwriting

❝Have a go at writing your own script.**❞**

Children can participate in scriptwriting whatever their age and level of literacy. It's a matter of tailoring the activity to suit your group. Within a setting with a wide age range, several different methods of developing scripts can operate at once, with different groups working in different ways. For instance:

- The children may work alone, collaborate with a partner or work within small groups.
- The children may develop a script consisting of lines of dialogue and stage directions, or they may briefly 'storyline' (outline) a plot to be improvised.
- Scripts and storylines can be as brief as a single scene or sketch, or as long as a full play – whatever suits the group.
- The children can make their own written notes and develop them into a storyline or script. Alternatively, they can work with an adult facilitator who helps to pull ideas together on the page.
- The children may write for different media, including puppet shows, stage performances, screen and radio.

Ways to develop scripts or storylines include the following.

Retelling a well-known story
Groups retell a well-known story, such as 'Red Riding Hood', in their own words. Ask how the story starts, then keep asking, 'What happens next?' You may challenge the children to come up with a different ending, or to update the plot (i.e. instead of stopping to pick flowers Red Riding Hood could stop to check her email on her laptop). These stories work well as puppet shows since the audience can easily follow the plot. They also work when individual scenes are acted out by different small groups in a drama workshop – simply allocate each small group a key scene to work on. Once everyone has had time to rehearse, call on each group in turn to perform their scene. This is a time-efficient way to act out a story from start to finish.

Playing the 'What happens next' game
Sit in a circle. Give the children an opening line, e.g. 'Ben thought it would be another ordinary day, but ...' The children should each take a turn to add a line to the story. Make a note of the storyline. It can be improvised or scripted later if desired.

Making up a new story for existing characters from books, TV or film

You may like to offer the children a starting point, e.g. 'What might happen if Tracy Beaker thought someone had stolen her MP3 player?' Again, this can be improvised or scripted later if desired.

Creating daydream monologues

Ask the children to think in the first person about something they daydream about, as if it's really happening, e.g. 'I can hear the roar of the crowd as I step onto the pitch ...' Encourage them to describe how they feel, and what they see, hear and taste. This can be written down and read/performed aloud, or spoken directly into a tape recorder and played to the group.

Acting out published scripts

There are numerous children's plays available to buy or borrow in book form. Many are short, and staging tips are included. These plays are generally suited to performance in front of an invited audience, should you wish to formally produce a play.

Writing to a format

Link
It's fun to recreate a TV or radio programme with a solid format. See 'Our own programme' on page 35.

✔ Good practice

Whatever activities you embark on, remember that children who don't want to perform can be in charge of scripts, props, costume and make-up, scenery/sets, prompting and, if you intend to invite people to watch a performance, even tickets and programmes.

Extension Idea

Older children may be ready for more of a challenge, and may even consider writing as a career. It's still a good idea for them to try writing an episode of an existing children's drama when starting out, as the plots tend to be less complicated than, say, a soap. Writing for an existing show eliminates the need to create characters and situations from scratch. The scripts can still be performed within the group.

 A professional scriptwriting template can be downloaded from the BBC Writersroom website, along with real scripts from children's TV dramas, which are a great learning tool, allowing older children to see how a TV story is both constructed and laid out on the page. Additional useful information can be found on the websites of many existing shows. For instance, the Tracy Beaker website has character profiles and storyline synopses which will help a budding screenwriter.

The BBC Blast site supports and encourages older children's scriptwriting, and offers the opportunity to have writing featured online. There's plenty of advice on getting started on your very first script. See page 40 for website details.

Showtime!

Our own programmes

"Be part of our 'TV' show!"

ACTIVITY

S P I C E

Equipment
- Notepads and pens
- Video camera/tape recording equipment
- Felt-tip pens
- Large pieces of paper
- Sticky-tack
- Costumes (optional)

Instructions

1. Choose a TV or radio programme format with which the group is familiar enough to make their own version, such as a particular quiz show or talent show. For our example, we'll take a typical quiz show.

2. Discuss and list the key features of the show:
   a) *Who is on screen?* In our example there will be a quiz master, six contestants and the audience.
   b) *What happens?* The quiz master introduces and talks to each contestant. In the first round, general knowledge questions are asked. The contestant with the lowest score is out. The one with the highest score can choose the category of questions to be asked in the next round. The choices are music, film, general knowledge and sport. This continues until there are two contestants left. There is an on-the-button quick-fire general knowledge round to establish the winner. The host invites the winner back next week and the show closes.

3. Consider what is done behind the scenes to create the show, i.e. there are camera operators, question researchers, link writers, set designers, etc.

4. Decide who will play each part and who will work on which behind-the-scenes job.

5. Create small groups to work on each task with adult support as appropriate, i.e. The set designers arrange the room layout and make a backdrop poster featuring the programme's name, the researchers devise questions and write them on cards. Camera operators practise filming angles, etc.

6. When everyone is ready, have a few run-throughs. The non-performers can become the audience, and can give constructive feedback.

7. Film a 'take'. You can edit if appropriate (optional).

8. Play the take on TV to watch your own show!

Link

✔ Good practice

Remember to get parental permission before filming/recording children. Also see the 'Photography and film' theme on page 1 and the 'Media' theme on page 109.

Link

Extension Idea

You may like to add an advertisement break (see below) and credits. See 'Roll the credits' on page 11.

Older children may like to parody an existing show, creating a comedy spoof.

Advertisements

"Make your own adverts and show them on 'TV'!"

ACTIVITY

SPICE

Equipment
- Bag
- Products (see below)
- Video camera or tape recorder (optional)

Instructions

1. Select a range of products for the children to advertise, and place items to represent them into a bag. Products could include a box of dog biscuits, tube of toothpaste, tin of baked beans, a toy, etc.

2. Have the children form pairs or small groups. Each pair/group should pull an item from the bag at random. They must act out a mock advert for the product they've chosen.

3. Allow time for planning and rehearsal.

4. Each group presents their advert in turn.

Extension Idea

You may like to video or tape record the adverts so the children can watch/listen to them. If you're making a mock TV or radio programme, the adverts can be played part-way through one after another to create an advertisement break.

ACTIVITY

Consequences

"Try out solutions to our problem scenarios.**"**

Equipment
- Slips of paper
- Pen

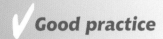

Instructions

1. On each piece of paper, write a realistic scenario which requires careful consideration, e.g. 'You've gone to a party. It's been arranged that your friend's mum will drop you home afterwards. But your friend doesn't turn up. What do you do?'
2. Have the children form small groups. Give each a scenario to consider.
3. Allow a few minutes for each group to decide what they should do in response to the scenario, and how they can act it out. (Not everyone in each group needs to perform.)
4. Allow group rehearsal time.
5. When ready, each group can then role-play their scenario to the whole group in turn.
6. Repeat with new scenarios if desired.

✔ Good practice

'Consequences' encourages children to think through issues connected with staying safe and behaving responsibly. Take time to talk children's responses through with them, particularly if they say they would do something inappropriate or unsafe.

Extension Idea

Older children can tackle more challenging scenarios suited to their age. For instance, 'You're offered drugs by someone waiting at the same bus stop as you. What do you do?'

Alternatively, two groups of older children can work on the same scenario. One group can do a 'best case scenario' version of how events could unfold, while the other group does a 'worst case scenario'.

Another variation of the activity is to write potentially funny scenarios, which include familiar characters. Older children can use these to create sketches by thinking through how the character would respond. Situations may include someone being late, misplacing a crucial item or forgetting something important. What would Mr Bean do? Or Superman? What chaos might ensue?

Puppet theatre

ACTIVITY

"Help to make a puppet theatre and put on a show!**"**

Many children who prefer not to perform directly in person enjoy expressing themselves via puppets. Making a group puppet theatre provides a platform.

Equipment
- Large rectangular cardboard box
- Stiff card (optional)
- Fabric remnants
- 2 lengths of ribbon
- Fringe
- Glue/stapler
- Poster paint and brushes
- Scissors
- Ruler and pencil

Instructions

1. If the box has flaps, cut them off.
2. Using a ruler, draw a rectangle on the base of the box as shown in the diagram below. Cut the rectangle out. The resulting gap represents the stage.
3. If you want to make the theatre more durable, cut stiff card to size and glue it to the inside of the box. Leave to dry.
4. Paint the theatre with poster paint. Leave to dry.
5. Cut a length of fringe to size and glue to the top of the stage opening, on the inside. Heavy fringing may require stapling.
6. Measure the length of the stage from the top of the opening to the bottom. Use this measurement to cut the fabric into two curtains of the appropriate size. Use pinking shears if possible to prevent fraying.
7. Fix one curtain to each side of the stage by gluing/stapling to the inside of the theatre.
8. Use a length of ribbon to tie back each curtain in the middle.

To use the theatre

Stand the theatre on a table. Puppeteers can sit behind the theatre to operate hand or finger puppets.

Link

- You can make 'photo figures' as described on page 9 into puppets – simply mount them on drinking straws.
- See page 90 for information about shadow puppets.
- See the website section on page 40 for more information on making puppets.

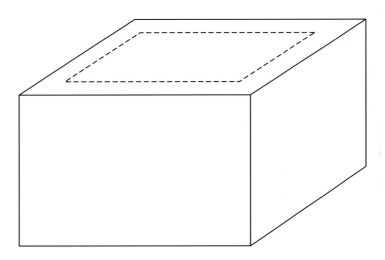

Cut out a rectangle to make a stage.

Puppet theatre

Websites

Visit:

www.familyfun.go.com/arts-and-crafts/sew/specialfeature/ craftgroups_puppets_sf/ for instructions on making a range of puppets

www.legendsandlore.com/after_pigsplay.html for ideas and advice on staging puppet shows. Includes a sample script

www.bbc.co.uk/cbbc/tracybeaker/index.shtml for information about the show 'The Story of Tracy Beaker'

www.bbc.co.uk/writersroom/ a site intended for adults that features a children's drama script archive and free scriptwriting Microsoft Word templates.

www.bbc.co.uk/blast/ for older children interested in the arts

4 The beach

Aspects of play

The beach is a broad theme full of possibilities. Activities can encompass traditional seaside pastimes, and explore life both on and under the ocean waves. Then there are mysterious treasure islands to think about ...

Children's experiences of the beach can differ greatly, depending on where they live and the opportunities they've had. While arranging a visit to the coast or a sea-life centre may not be possible for all groups, every setting can bring the essence of the seaside to the children with a bit of imagination. For instance, you can make a small play beach by laying a large tarpaulin on the floor and putting down as much play sand as practical. Add some shells, pebbles, deck chairs, buckets and spades. Liven up the sandpit by topping it up with water to create an 'ocean bed' for paddling in. You can even play a beach sound effect CD in the background.

You may like to invite some visitors to speak to the group. For instance, coastguards and lifeguards promote beach/swimming safety to groups, and children can be fascinated by someone willing to share their experience of activities such as deep-sea diving.

Resources to support free play

- Play sand
- Shells
- Pebbles
- Sand toys such as buckets, spades and moulds
- Water
- Large cardboard boxes to be used as boats in role play by younger children (and also used in the 'Wavers and throwers' game outlined on page 47)
- Beach sound effects CD

Sand sculptures

"You can make everlasting sandcastles and sculptures with our special sand dough.**"**

Equipment

- 4 cups play sand
- 2 cups cornflour
- 1 heaped tablespoon cream of tartar
- 3 cups warm water
- Mixing bowl
- Wooden spoon
- PVA glue
- Glue brush

Instructions

1. The children mix the dry ingredients together in the bowl.
2. Slowly stir in the water bit by bit. When the mixture becomes too hard to stir, discard the spoon and mix by hand.
3. Remove the dough and kneed until it holds together well.
4. The dough can now be used for modelling. When children have made their sculptures, place them on a warm window sill to set for a couple of days.
5. When set, the models can be varnished for posterity with a solution of PVA glue and water, mixed in equal quantities and applied with a glue brush. Leave to dry thoroughly.

Flapper fish

"Make a colourful flapper fish and enter our under-the-ocean race!**"**

Equipment

- Card
- Pencils
- Scissors
- Thin paper
- Felt tip pens
- Newspaper

Instructions

1. Draw a fish approximately 30 cm long on a piece of card. Cut it out to make a fish template.
2. The children trace around the template onto thin paper, then cut out their own fish shape. The fish can be decorated with felt-tips.
3. The children can make their fish flap across the floor by fanning them from behind with a folded newspaper. Give them time to practise, then hold fish flapping races. (The template ensures the races are fair since all fish are the same size.)

Don't rock the boat

"Don't rock the boat in this game or your team will capsize!"

ACTIVITY

S P I C E

Equipment
● Chalk

Instructions

Reminder: bow = front of boat, stern = back, port = left, starboard = right

1. Split the children into teams of an even number, e.g. six. Each team should sit one behind the other in a line.
2. Draw the chalk outline of a boat around each team, so it seems as though each team is sitting in their own boat. Leave a gap of about 25 cm between the children and the chalk outline.
3. To start play, shout out 'All aboard!' On this signal, the child at the bow of each boat (position 1) and the child at the stern of each boat (position 6) must swap places. Those in position 1 should stand up and hurry towards the stern, moving down the port side of the boat. At the same time position 6s should make their way to the bow, moving up the starboard side. The players must be careful not to step out over the chalk outline since this will 'rock the boat'.
4. When a team rocks their boat an adult should call out 'Capsized!' Both children must freeze for a 5-second penalty before continuing.
5. Once the children are seated, the players in positions 2 and 5 must swap places in the same way, followed by the children in positions 3 and 4.
6. When everyone has swapped positions, the team must call out in unison 'Land ahoy!' The first team to do so wins the game.

Ice-cream in-a-bag

"Shake to make your own delicious soft ice-cream, just like you'd have at the beach!**"**

Equipment
- Zip lock food bags
- Granulated sugar
- Milk
- Vanilla essence
- Rock salt
- Ice cubes

Instructions

The amounts given are sufficient for one ice-cream. Adjust the recipe as necessary. You can re-use the bags and rock salt to make several ice-creams.

1. The zip-lock food bags must be at least the 570 ml (1 pint) size. The children should fill one bag with half a cup of milk, 1 tablespoon of sugar and a single drop of vanilla essence. Seal the bag securely.
2. Place the sealed bag inside a second zip-lock bag, and add the rock-salt (to the second bag).
3. Top up the second bag with ice cubes, then seal it securely.
4. The children should shake their bag vigorously. After 5–10 minutes of shaking they will have delicious soft ice-cream in their bag. Turn it out into a bowl and enjoy!

Shark attack

"Look out, there'll be sharks about in our fun parachute game!**"**

Equipment
- Parachute

Instructions

1. Place the parachute on the floor.
2. The children sit around the parachute with their legs underneath.

3. Choose a volunteer to be the shark. He or she should go under the parachute and begin swimming (crawling) around.

4. The other players billow the parachute furiously to create waves that hide the shark from view. It's fun to chant the well known 'Jaws' theme tune too – 'Da-da! Da-da! Da-da, da-da ...' etc!

5. The shark eventually taps someone on the leg. That person now slides (generally screaming dramatically!) beneath the waves, where they also become a shark.

6. The billowing of waves continues. The new shark now taps someone else on the leg, while the old shark continues swimming.

7. The game continues in this way until there are more sharks than players. The players left are the winners.

Parachute games are popular

Treasure chest

ACTIVITY

S P I C E

"Need somewhere to hide your secret treasure? Make a shell chest to take home..."

Equipment
- Craft shells
- Small containers (see below)
- Plaster of Paris
- Palette knife
- Play sand

Instructions
1. The children choose a small trinket-size container to work with, such as an empty stock cube box or a margarine container.
2. Make up a stiff mixture of plaster of Paris according to the directions on the packet.
3. Use the palette knife to smear the sides and lid of the container with the mixture.
4. Push shells into the wet plaster of Paris.
5. Sprinkle sand into the gaps and shake off the excess. Leave to dry.

Extension Idea

Older children may like to use this technique to create a shell vase, which makes a good gift. Simply swap the container for a jam jar. When dry, the vase should be sprayed with waterproof non-toxic varnish.

✔ Good practice

Don't dispose of leftover plaster of Paris down the sink – it blocks the pipes. Have the children scrape the excess from their hands into the bin before washing them.

Wavers and throwers

"Will your team win our fast-paced beach game?"

Equipment

- Pieces of stiff card approximately 75 cm square
- Pencils
- Scissors
- Soft tennis balls or newspaper balls
- 2 'boats' (cardboard boxes)
- Chalk

Instructions

1. Half the children in the group will need cardboard waves. Working in pairs to create one set of waves between them, the children draw a wave shape onto their piece of card and cut it out. (A large cardboard box opened out would suffice.)

2. Take two large-scale model boats (boxes) and place them facing each other several metres apart – the distance apart will depend on your group and how far the children can throw on average, so use your judgement. Draw a chalk line down the middle of the playground to show where each team's playing space begins and ends.

3. Divide the group into two teams and allocate a boat to each – these will be the team's bases.

4. Label half of each team as 'wavers', and the remaining half as 'throwers'.

5. The wavers should spread out in front of their team's boat, equipped with a cardboard wave each. The throwers should stand a few paces in front of the wavers, equipped with several soft tennis balls each. (You can use scrunched up newspaper balls as an alternative, but you may need to move the boats closer together.)

6. Simultaneously on your signal, the throwers from each team must try to throw as many balls as possible into the opposing team's boat, while the wavers defend their boat by trying to deflect the balls with their waves.

7. The throwers may pick up and make use of any balls that miss or are deflected, but balls successfully thrown into a boat cannot be removed. The wavers can only deflect balls, they may not throw them, but throwers can deflect or catch any balls that come their way. Throwers may move around but must not cross the chalk line.

▶

8. This game is exciting and fast-paced and adults will need to keep a careful eye to ensure the rules are observed as the balls fly overhead!

9. You can either set a time limit for the duration of the game (i.e. 10 minutes) or allow the game to continue until the balls have run out. Count up the number of balls in each boat. The team with the least balls in their own boat wins.

Link Also see the 'Walking the plank' trust game on page 96.

Surf safari

"Make your own cool surfboard to play with, and practise your surfing moves!"

ACTIVITY

SPICE

Equipment
- Large pieces of stiff card
- Images/clips of surfboards and surfers
- Pencils
- Paint/felt-tip pens
- Stereo and music

Instructions

1. Show the children pictures of surfers and surfboards sourced from books/magazines/the internet. You may also like to show video/DVD clips of surfers in action.

2. Each child should draw a surfboard shape onto a piece of large piece of stiff card (a large cardboard box opened out would suffice). This can be drawn freehand, but you can make a template from a real surfboard if you have access to one.

3. Inspired by the images/clips, the children can draw some colourful designs onto their boards, paint/colour them and leave them to dry.

4. There are several things to do with the finished boards. Some children enjoy role playing with their boards, pretending to ride the waves and do the stunts and tricks they have seen. Why not supply some surfing music to get them in the mood? Some children simply enjoy strolling around with their board under their arm, looking cool! The boards also make an eye-catching wall display when grouped together. The children may like to display them with the cardboard waves made for the 'Wavers and throwers' game which can be painted. They could add a few surfers too.

Extension Idea

A whole culture has grown up around surfing in the UK in recent years, which is likely to interest older children. They may enjoy making their own surf-style clothing designs, and even graphic designs for the bodywork of the iconic campervan. This can be done on paper or using computer programs (see the website section on page 53). To give them the opportunity to realise their designs, why not ask children to bring in an item of clothing, such as a plain T-shirt, to customise with fabric paints?

You may be able to invite a surfer to talk to the group about the sport, and perhaps give tips on how children interested in water sports can get started locally. Even if you're too far from the coast for surfing classes, the local swimming pool may offer scuba-diving lessons.

Surf's up!

ACTIVITY

Captain's coming

"Can you think of any new moves for this traditional game?"

S P I C E

Instructions

1. Choose a volunteer to stand at the front of the group. Their job is to call out instructions to the rest of the children. The players must do the corresponding action until the next instruction is given.
2. The last child to comply with each instruction is out. Anyone who does the wrong action is also out.
3. The last child remaining is the winner.
4. The instructions and corresponding actions are:
   - Captain's coming = salute
   - Bow = run to the front of the play space
   - Stern = run to the back
   - Starboard = run to the right
   - Port = run to the left
   - Scrub the decks = hands and knees to mime scrubbing the floor
   - Climb the rigging = mime climbing upwards
   - Sharks = lie down and snap arms together in the manner of jaws
   - Submarines = lie down on back with one leg in the air as a periscope
   - Man overboard = mime throwing a lifeline
5. Ask the children to suggest their own additional instructions and actions.

Jelly vessels

"Fun to make and delicious to eat!"

Equipment
- Oranges
- Sharp knife
- Tablespoon
- Squeezer
- Orange quickset jelly and water
- Cocktail sticks
- Paper plates
- Icing
- Paper
- Scissors
- Felt-tip pens
- Sticky tape

Instructions

1. Each child needs half an orange, so cut the fruit in half.
2. The children should squeeze the juice from their orange, and retain it.
3. Use a spoon to scrape out the inside of the orange and discard it.
4. Make up the jelly firmly according to the instructions, but replace a little of the water with the orange juice for flavour.
5. Pour the jelly into the orange halves and put them in the fridge to set.
6. Meanwhile, pipe a decorative wave designs onto the plates with icing and leave it to set. You can buy a tube of ready-made icing that comes with a piping nozzle or make your own with icing sugar and water, to be used in a piping bag.
7. Cut two triangular sails from paper, decorate them with felt-tips and stick each one to a cocktail stick mast. (The sail should come no more than three-quarters of the way down the stick.)
8. When the jelly is set, slice the orange halves into quarters to make two boat shapes. Place the boats on the plate. Add the final flourish by pushing masts into the jelly, one per boat.

✔ Good practice

Most older children will be able to cut fruit independently and make up jelly themselves. For safety, younger children will need close supervision or to have the tasks done for them, depending on their age and ability.

Floating origami boats

S P I C E

"Make paper boats that really float!"

Equipment
- Card rectangles
- Pencils
- Ruler
- Scissors
- Sticky tape

Instructions

Also see the diagram on the page opposite.

1. Take a rectangle of card and draw a circle at each end. Draw a dot in the middle of each circle.

2. Draw a straight line from the top of the first circle to the top of the second circle.

3. Draw a straight line from the bottom of the first circle to the bottom of the second circle. This creates a cylinder-like shape.

4. To create the sides of the boat, crease the sides of the cylinder upwards about 5 mm in from the edge on either side.

5. Cut a slit into one of the circles, stopping at the dot. To make a curved bow, overlap the cut edges (as you would if making a paper cone) and stick them together.

6. Repeat at the other end to make the stern.

7. The boat will float in water. It can be pushed or blown along with a straw.

The children can try adapting the basic design to create different boats. Varying the size and number of circles and their distance apart alters the size and shape of the boats. For instance, two small circles a long way apart will create a thin barge. Three circles in a triangle shape will make a speedboat, and two circles at each end will create a square cargo carrier.

Extension Idea

Older children may like to learn how to make a range of more complicated origami sea creatures and boats. You can download patterns from the internet – see the websites section on page 53.

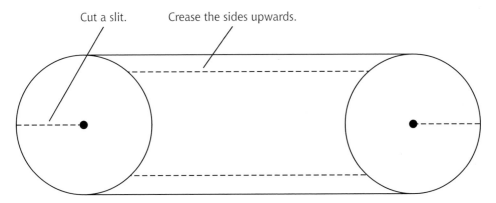

Cut a slit.   Crease the sides upwards.

Floating origami boats

Websites

Visit:

www.beachsafety.org.uk/bs/home/default.asp the site of the RNLI Beach Lifeguards; includes safety fact sheets and a fun online safety game

www.123child.com/UBB/showthread.php?t=3041 for beach activities for younger children

www.enchantedlearning.com/subjects/ocean/ for facts about the ocean, printouts and quizzes

www.enchantedlearning.com/crafts/origami/whale/ and **www. activityvillage.co.uk/origami_for_kids.htm** for origami patterns suitable for older children

www.bbc.co.uk/cbbc/art/howto/fashion/ for fashion design tips and printable templates suitable for older children

5 The fairground

Aspects of play

With traditional fairground sideshows dying out, many children have never taken aim on a coconut shy or hooked a duck. Yet these activities prove to be as popular as ever when children have the chance to try them. This theme combines traditional sideshows with modern ideas, and reflects all the fun of the fair.

You might like to offer one or two different sideshows per session, alternating them over time. Or, you may prefer to set out all the sideshows at once, turning the setting into a fairground environment temporarily.

You'll want to give children unlimited goes on each sideshow. But this raises the issue of what to do about prizes, the provision of which cannot be endless. I suggest buying a large book of raffle tickets. Each time a child wins, hand them a ticket and have them write their name on the back. Place the tickets in a large container. At the end of the theme, draw out one winning ticket. The more tickets a child earns the more chances they'll have of winning. Oversized soft toys make a great traditional fairground prize. You can also offer an inexpensive novelty for everyone with a ticket in the jar, so nobody goes away empty handed.

If you're working with older children, you might like to give them the opportunity to set up and run sideshows as a community fundraising event. By charging a small fee per go and offering small prizes, they can raise money for their own setting or for a nominated charity. Set an age limit on some of the easier shows to win on, or adults visiting your event may clean you out of prizes! You'll need to ensure that children are closely supervised when dealing with the public. Carefully consider how the event will be organised – a book such as *Tried and Tested Ideas for Local Fundraising Events* by Sarah Passingham (ISBN 1903991374) will give you the practical and legal knowledge to run an event successfully.

Resources to support free play

- Play money
- Raffle tickets
- Internet access
- Fairground-related fiction and non-fiction books
- Pictures of fairground art

SPICE

Coconut shy

"Roll up, roll up to knock down a coconut!"

Equipment
- Table
- 4 coconuts
- 4 tall plastic beakers
- 3 tennis balls
- Chalk

Instructions

1. Assign one child or more to run or assist in running the sideshow.

2. Put four tall plastic beakers on a table and place a coconut on each one. Position the beakers a good distance apart so players have to aim at individual targets.

3. Using your judgement to make the game challenging but not impossible, draw a chalk line for children to stand behind when they take aim. In groups of a wide age range you may like to draw two lines so that younger children can stand closer to the table and older children further away.

4. Each child has three tennis balls per turn to throw at the coconuts. They must knock a coconut clean off the table to win.

✔ Good practice

This game needs plenty of clear space, and is best played outside if possible. Set up the table in front of a wall, so no one will walk behind the sideshow. This ensures passers-by won't be hit by a heavy coconut. For the same reason, instruct the children running the sideshow not to reposition coconuts or retrieve tennis balls until each player has thrown all three of their balls. They should stand well clear while players have their turn.

Roll up, roll up!

Bottle hoopla

*"*Can you hoopla a bottle to win?
It's not as easy as it sounds!*"*

Equipment
- Table
- 60+ empty plastic drink bottles
- Play sand or water
- Funnel
- Parcel tape
- Hoops
- Chalk

Instructions
1. You need to collect together as many plastic drink bottles as possible – 60 plus is ideal. This needn't be difficult if you ask the local café to help you out. The bottles should be of the same height and shape – 250 ml fizzy drink bottles are ideal.

2. Use a funnel to pour a little play sand in the bottom of each bottle to weight it down. If you only intend to use the hoopla for one day, you can use water instead.

3. Place the bottles side by side on the table to form a square grid. The bottles should be touching. Wrap some parcel tape around the outside of the whole grid to keep it together – this requires several pairs of hands. Taping the bottles together makes the sideshow challenging as hoops will frequently bounce off the bottles.

4. You'll need three small hoops approximately 7–8 cm in diameter for the children to throw over the bottles. You can improvise to make use of whatever you have to hand. Scrap stores often stock suitable objects. Plastic hoops (such as plastic sticky-tape inserts) will bounce off bottles well. Cardboard ones will make the game easier.

5. Draw a chalk line for players to stand behind.

6. Assign one child or more to run or assist in running the sideshow. Allow each player three shots per turn. Players must keep both feet on the ground when throwing.

Whack-a-ball

" You'll need good timing to whack a ball when you can't see it coming ... "

ACTIVITY

Equipment
- Long length of tube (see below)
- Balls
- Cricket bat

Instructions

1. You need a tube of at least 2 m in length. A new piece of down pipe guttering is ideal, but you can improvise by using the inner cardboard tube from a large roll of paper or carpet, or something similar. (Your local carpet shop will probably be able to help you.)

2. Assign one child or more to run or assist in running the sideshow. They can either hold the tube at a 45° angle (with the bottom on the floor), or the tube can be propped up.

3. The player should be equipped with the cricket bat, and must wait three paces back from the bottom end of the tube with their bat poised.

▶

4. One child should place a tennis ball in the top end of the tube, and shout 'Now!' as they let it go.

5. The player should attempt to hit the ball with the cricket bat as it comes out of the tube. The ball must be hit in one swing to count as a win.

Extension Idea

There are several ways to make this sideshow more challenging for older children, although it's a good idea to give them a chance to master the original game first, which is not as easy as it sounds. Try holding the tube at a steeper angle to speed up the exit of the ball, or have the player stand further away. You can change the rules so that players must stop the ball instead of hitting it, or you can replace the tennis ball with a smaller rubber jet-ball (high-bounce ball) so the exit is unpredictable.

Marble challenge

"Is your hand steady enough for our tricky marble challenge?"

ACTIVITY

S P I C E

Equipment
- Table
- Tray
- Plant pot (see below)
- Marbles
- Teaspoon
- Stopwatch
- Paper and pen

Instructions

1. Assign one child or more to run or assist in running the sideshow.

2. This activity requires a plant pot with a hole in the bottom big enough for a marble to pass through. Position the plant pot upside down in the middle of a tray, and place the tray on the table.

3. Tip a bag of marbles out onto the tray, so they surround the plant pot.

4. The player must hold the teaspoon in their preferred hand, and place their other hand behind their back.

5. The child running the side-show should set the stopwatch for 1 minute. On their signal, the player should begin using the teaspoon to scoop up the marbles one by one and drop them through the hole in the plant pot, continuing until their time is up.

6. A note should be made of the player's score. At the end of the session, award a prize for highest number of marbles scored. You may like to divide the competition into age categories.

Extension Idea

Challenge older children to attempt the task using their non-preferred hand, so right-handed children use their left hand and vice-versa.

Hook-a-duck

"Get quacking to hook-a-duck in this fairground favourite!**"**

Equipment
- 6+ rubber ducks
- Hook and eyes
- Garden canes
- Sandpaper
- Water tray/paddling pool
- Water
- Chalk

Instructions

This sideshow does take some preparation but it's worth the effort. Once you have the resources you can make the activity available as part of free play at any time.

1. You can buy metal hooks and eyes in various sizes from hardware stores. To make each duck 'hookable', screw a metal eye into the head of each duck. The smaller the hooks, the more difficult the game will be. Don't use heavyweight hooks as these capsize the ducks! You may find you need to make a small hole first with a nail-punch.

2. To make a rod, screw a hook into the end of a garden cane. Sand the other end lightly with sandpaper to get rid of splinters. Repeat until you have the desired number of rods.

3. Place a paddling pool or water tray on the floor and fill with water. The game is too easy if a water tray is used on a stand. Paddling pools should be well-filled to ensure the children don't pierce the bottom when they miss a duck.

4. Draw a chalk circle around the pool which players must stand behind.

5. The children can now attempt to hook the ducks. You may want to limit the number of attempts each player can have each turn, or apply a time limit per go.

Younger children may like to make a hook-a-fish game to take home – see the websites section on page 65 for a pattern.

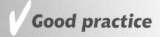 **Good practice**

Younger children will need some help to make the ducks and rods. Ensure an adult supervises the water, even if children run the side-show.

 **Extension Idea**

For older children, you may like to vary the size of the hooks and eyes to make some ducks/rods more difficult to work with.

 ## Chopstick challenge

"Can you transport slippery jellybeans using only chopsticks?**"**

ACTIVITY

Equipment

- Chopsticks
- 2 dishes
- Jellybeans

- Stopwatch
- Kitchen foil squares

Instructions

1. Fill a dish with jellybeans and place on a table alongside an empty dish and a pair of chopsticks.

2. Set the stopwatch for 2 minutes. On the start signal, the player must pick up the chopsticks and use them to move as many jellybeans as they can to the empty dish. They can hold and manipulate the chopsticks anyway they like, using one or both hands.

3. A note should be made of the player's score. At the end of the session, award a prize for highest number of jellybeans scored. You may like to divide the competition into age categories.

4. Alternatively, you may like to allow the children a shorter amount of time and give them the jellybeans they win. Have some kitchen foil squares handy. Tip the jellybeans won onto the foil, twist the foil around them and hand to the player.

Additional inspiration

The resources available to you can inspire additional sideshows. You may have skittles for instance, or large hoops that inspire a giant hoopla. Encourage the children to be creative.

All the fun of the fair

ACTIVITY

SP!CE

Sweet stall

"No fair is complete without the sweet stall. Help us to make some delicious treats to share!"

Fairground fudge

Equipment
- Microwave
- 1 400 g tin sweetened condensed milk (not evaporated)
- 1 pack chocolate chips
- 1 teaspoon vanilla essence
- 20 cm sandwich tin
- Kitchen foil
- Bowl
- Spoon
- Knife
- Margarine

Instructions
1. Line the tin with foil. Use plenty so the foil extends over the sides of the tin. Grease the foil lightly with margarine.
2. Mix the condensed milk and chocolate chips in a microwavable bowl.
3. Microwave on HIGH until melted (approximately 1½ minutes), stirring once during cooking.
4. Remove from the microwave and stir until smooth.
5. Stir in the vanilla essence
6. Pour into the tin. Place in the fridge to set for at least 2 hours.
7. Lift the ends of the foil to remove the fudge from the tin. Then peel the foil from the fudge.
8. Cut the fudge into squares with a sharp knife. Store in an airtight container in the fridge.

Toffee apples
This recipe is suitable for older children working with direct supervision. In a mixed age setting children can collaborate. Younger children could complete steps 1, 2, 3, 4 and 10, while older children are responsible for steps 5–9.

Equipment

- 15 small red apples
- 3 cups sugar
- 1 cup water
- 1 teaspoon vinegar
- Lollipop sticks
- Baking sheet
- Kitchen foil
- Cellophane squares
- String
- Scissors

Instructions

1. Wash the apples and dry them thoroughly.
2. Remove the stems. Push the lollipop sticks into the stem end of the apple.
3. Chill in the fridge for an hour. (Later when the hot toffee meets the cold apples it will set immediately.)
4. Line the baking tray with foil.
5. Mix the sugar, water and vinegar in a saucepan. Bring slowly to the boil, stirring constantly. Ensure the sugar completely dissolves before the mixture reaches boiling point.
6. Simmer the toffee until it thickens and turns a deep golden colour, stirring constantly.
7. To test if the toffee is done, drop a small amount from the spoon into a beaker of cold water – it should form a hard ball. When done, remove from the heat without delay.
8. Holding by the stick, dip the apples into the toffee. Twirl them around to coat them well. Allow the excess to drip back into the saucepan.
9. Stand the coated apples on their ends on the baking trays to set. Don't put toffee apples in the fridge or they will go sticky.
10. When completely cold, the toffee apples can be wrapped in squares of cellophane, and tied with a string bow.

Popcorn

You may also like to buy some popping corn and make it up according to the directions on the packet.

Bumper car skipping

" Test your skipping skills with this bumper car rhyme. **"**

Equipment
- Skipping rope

Instructions

1. Two children should twirl the skipping rope. The skipper should jump in when ready, which is the cue for the twirlers to recite the following rhyme:

   > Bumper car, bumper car,
   > Number forty-eight,
   > Went round the corrr-ner,
   > And slammed on the BRAKES!

2. When the children start to say 'corner', the skipper must jump out of the swing of the rope, run around one of the twirlers and then jump back in on the opposite side of the rope. The twirlers can't finish saying the word 'corner' until the player is back in, and so they must continue to make the 'corrr' sound for a few seconds before making the 'ner' sound.

3. The twirlers should shout the word 'brakes'. On this signal the skipper must attempt to land directly on the rope, stopping the swing.

Fairground art

There is a long tradition of art in fairgrounds, the function of which is to provide a colourful, bold backdrop to rides and side-shows. Antique fairground art is treasured and displayed in museums. Some fairs have restored beautifully painted antique carousels, and these take pride of place in their fairgrounds. The contemporary trend is for airbrushed fairground art. Impressive, stylised effects can be achieved. See the website section on page 65 for sites where children can view both airbrushed and traditional fairground art.

Extension Idea

Older children can create their own designs and try their hand at airbrushing. Airbrushes are available from art supply stores, with prices starting at about £25. You can also purchase kits which allow children to 'air blow' ink from felt-tip pens, producing a less sophisticated and less predictable result, but allowing the technique to be explored for around £10.

Why not arrange an airbrush artist to visit your setting and demonstrate the techniques of the craft? You may find an airbrush artist at an art college, sign writing centre, model shop or a garage offering custom bodywork for vehicles.

Websites

Visit:

www.library.thinkquest.org/C002926/home.html for fairground history and information about how rides work. Includes colouring pages for younger children. Older children can do quizzes and participate in creative writing by finishing fairground stories and posting them online

www.fairgroundart.co.uk/pages/default.htm for traditional, contemporary and antique fairground art

www.airbrushartuk.com/kevweb/fairground/index.htm for contemporary airbrushed fairground art

www.microprizes.com/index.htm for online games. Younger children can win virtual goldfish, control ferris wheels and play bumper cars

www.wondertime.go.com/create-and-play/cutting-pages. html?CMP=KNC-BT3727858078 click on 'Gone fishing' to download and print out a hook-a-fish game for younger children to make and take home

6 Music

Aspects of play

There are many different types of music, and numerous ways in which to experience them all. This includes making music, listening to live and recorded music, singing, song writing, dancing and games.

During the theme, you can provide access to familiar music favoured by the children, as well as taking the opportunity to introduce the group to music from different genres – from classical to country, and from rock to reggae. Music from different decades and countries can also be explored.

The enjoyment of music is subjective. Individual children will have their own tastes and opinions about what they hear and choose to listen to. That's a good thing – it means there will be a melting pot of musical ideas and preferences to draw from during the activities. Like music, this theme can be shared by everyone, but interpreted by children individually.

Resources to support free play

- Stereo
- Recorded music
- Music videos/DVDs
- Television
- Video/DVD recorder/player
- Musical instruments
- Microphones
- Craft resources
- Books/magazines
- Dressing up resources
- Internet access

Stage name game

"Create your own celebrity pop persona!"

ACTIVITY

Instructions

1. All players sit in a circle.

2. Ask each player to think of either a song title or the name of a group that starts with the same letter as their own first name. They then adopt this as their last name, to give them their stage name. For instance, naming herself after a song title, a child called Sarah may choose the stage name 'Sarah Smile'. A child naming themselves after a group may become 'Michael McFly'.

3. When everyone has decided on a name, one child should be selected to introduce themselves to the group – 'I'm Sarah Smile.'

4. The next player must repeat the previous player's name, and then introduce themselves – 'That's Sarah Smile, and I'm Michael McFly.' ▶

5. The third player has to remember two names before introducing themselves – 'That's Sarah Smile, that's Michael McFly, and I'm Ollie Ordinary Boys.' Continue in the same way around the circle, until everyone has had a turn. (It's a good idea to sit younger children together and begin with them, so they have less to remember. They can always have a go at remembering more names at the end of the game if they'd like the challenge.)

6. If a child becomes stuck when trying to recall a name, they can be given a musical clue. The song in question could be hummed for instance, or the lead singer of a band could be revealed.

ACTIVITY

Song writing

❝ Help write lyrics to create a cool club song. **❞**

Equipment
- Music to listen to
- Paper and pens

Instructions

1. The purpose of the activity is to come up with a song that represents the setting. For ease of explanation, we'll take an out-of-school club writing a club song as our example.

2. Together, word storm the aspects of the club that the children would like to mention in the song. For instance, popular activities, such as playing games or going on trips, or the fact that club members make new friends when they attend.

3. Decide how the group will work. Children often choose to collaborate in pairs or small groups, but some may prefer to work alone.

4. Encourage each group to select a tune they all know. This can be a pop song, traditional tune or even a jingle.

5. The children write lyrics featuring some of the key points discussed in the word-storming process. See below for an example of lyrics written by a group to the tune of 'Princess Pat', see page 69.

6. Give each group the opportunity to practise and perform their song.

Playtime Club Song

If you want to have fun,
Playtime is the place to come,
'Cos it's really cool,
And there's loads to do.
You can make new friends,
And play cool games,
And there's a prize bin,
Full of things you can win.

Before school,
And after school too,
And in the holidays,
You can stay all day.
So join our club,
And you will see,
That Playtime is …
A great place to be!

Extension Idea

Older children can extend favourite songs with an extra verse or two in keeping with the original lyrics. They can also write and perform their own original music – how this is achieved will depend on the experience of the group. It's well worth arranging for a local expert to run a song writing/music making workshop for older children. The Youth Music organisation has regional workers who can help with networking – see the website section on page 78 for further details.

Musical circles

❝This game will have you dancing in circles, but can you run rings around the opposition?❞

ACTIVITY

SP☐CE

Equipment
- Stereo
- Music

▶

Instructions

1. Ask the children to form pairs, and to decide who will be referred to as 'number 1' and who will be 'number 2' for the duration of the game.

2. All the 1s should form a circle, facing outwards. All the 2s should form an outer circle surrounding the 1s, facing inwards. At the start of the game, each child should be facing their partner, within their respective circles.

3. When music is played, the 1s should move clockwise in their circle, while the 2s move anti-clockwise.

4. Stop the music at regular intervals. Each time, shout out two body parts, for example, 'elbow and foot!' The children must run to find their partner. They must then make contact with their relevant body parts, holding the position until the music starts again. The last pair in position, and any pairs unable to hold their position, are out.

'Bird on a perch' (see below) is a variation of this game.

Extension Idea

You can make 'Musical circles' more complicated for older players by adding an additional rule that the body part called out first applies to the number 1s, and the body part called second applies to the number 2s. So in our example, the number 1s would have to use their elbow to make contact with their partner's foot. Pairs who get this the wrong way around are also out.

Bird on a perch

"Can you make it 'home' in time to stay in the game?"

ACTIVITY

SP🎲CE

Equipment
● Stereo
● Music

Instructions

1. Ask the children to form pairs. One child in each pair should be the 'bird', and the other should be the 'perch'.

2. The birds should form a circle, facing inwards.

3. The perches should form an outer circle surrounding the birds, facing inwards.

4. When music is played, the birds should walk clockwise in their circle, while the perches walk anti-clockwise. Upbeat music with a quick tempo complements this game.

5. Stop the music at regular intervals. This is the signal for the perches to kneel on one knee, making a 'perch' with their other leg. The birds must run to their partner and sit on the perch. In each round, the last pair to get into position is out.

6. Once the children have the hang of the game, ask them to move briskly in their circles, dancing or jogging in time to the music.

7. The game is over when there is one winning pair left. Give the birds and perches the opportunity to swap roles, then play a second round.

Name that tune

"Test your musical knowledge in this fun team quiz."

ACTIVITY

Equipment

S P I C E

- Stereo
- Music
- Paper and pens

Instructions

1. Split the group into teams, ideally groups of five or six. Elect a team captain, and equip the captain with a pen and paper.

2. As in the old television programme of the same name, the aim of the game is to name the title of a song, just from hearing the introduction. When playing with younger children, it works well to play the first few seconds of well-known pop songs. When the music is stopped, allow the teams a few seconds to confer, then ask the captains to write down their answer. At the end of the game, the answers can be marked, and points awarded for each answer. You may like to award extra points if teams can name the artist as well as the title.

Extension Idea

If playing with older children, you can follow the more complicated instructions below, and use a broader range of music, including older songs.

Equipment
● Stopwatch

Instructions

1. Before playing a song, give the children some basic information about it, for instance, the genre (pop, rap, etc.), and perhaps the decade (current, nineties, etc.).

2. Throughout the game teams can confer, but to avoid confusion and shouting out, answers must come via the team captains. Based on the information given about the song, one team must make a bid in seconds of how soon they believe they can recognise the tune – for instance, 45 seconds. The highest acceptable bid of time should be 60 seconds, and the lowest 2 seconds.

3. The other teams now have an opportunity to make their own lower bid. This continues until the teams drop out of the bidding one by one (unwilling to bid any lower), or until one team bids 2 seconds.

4. The music should be played for the team who won the bidding for the appropriate number of seconds, in our example 20 seconds. The team then has 30 seconds to confer, at the end of which the captain should attempt to 'name that tune'.

5. If they answer correctly, the team wins three points. The bidding for a new song should then start – a different team should start the bidding in the new round.

6. However, if they answer incorrectly, the team is now out of the round, and cannot guess again. The song should be played again for the remaining teams who may confer. The first team captain to raise their hand can attempt to name the tune. If they are correct, the team wins one point. If they are incorrect, the team is out of the round, and the music should be played again until one team answers correctly, or until the remaining teams pass.

7. The team with the most points wins. You may like to offer small prizes.

Dance routines

ACTIVITY

SPICE

" *Show us your moves and learn some new ones in our dance-'til-you-drop workshop!* **"**

Equipment
- Stereo
- Music
- Television
- Videos/DVDs

Instructions

Children often enjoy both learning dance routines and choreographing their own. You can run 'dance workshops' in a number of ways:

- Some children (and/or staff) may already know dance moves to certain pop songs, and may be willing to teach them to other children in their own dance workshop.
- You can use instructional videos hired from the library to teach children some basic dance steps in various genres – simple line dancing routines and salsa moves can be effectively learnt in this way, for instance.
- The children can pick a favourite piece of music and choreograph dance moves into their own routine. Younger children may enjoy devising steps in pairs or groups, with everyone performing the same steps at the same time.
- Don't forget the ever popular disco. A few flashing lights and some music and you're ready to go. Flashing lights are incorporated into many children's stereos, and simple children's disco balls can be purchased cheaply.

Extension Idea

Older children may like a more complicated dance troupe routine, which involves staggered timings (as in a Mexican wave – everyone does the same move in a sequence), or formations. Alternatively, older children may appreciate a real DJ deck (which can be borrowed or hired), and the opportunity to take turns to DJ.

Dancing the conga

✓ Good practice

Before embarking on a dance workshop, ensure the children warm up their bodies sufficiently, and include winding down exercises at the end of the session. Unless you're suitably trained in teaching dance safely to children, you should stick to teaching simple, low risk movements from which injury is unlikely. There can still be plenty of challenge involved in making these into a routine, and performing them in time to music.

You could bring in an expert visitor if you wish to offer movements or genres which have a higher degree of risk. It's important to note that the level of risk alters depending on the experience and competence of the individual children participating. It's well worth arranging for groups to see live dancing if possible, which might entail going on a trip or having a visit from professionals. There's something dynamic about watching live dance that doesn't transfer to the screen.

Don't use flashing lights if the children have conditions such as epilepsy that can be triggered by their effects.

Stars in their eyes

"Your chance to dress like a star for our club photoshoot! Get ready for your close-up!"

Equipment
- Dressing up clothes
- Accessories including dress jewellery, shades and hats
- Mirror
- Hair styling accessories, such as gel
- Face paints
- Pictures of pop stars (magazines/posters, etc.)
- Camera

Instructions

Fashion and music go hand in hand, so give the children a mirror to look in and plenty of clothes and accessories to try on, and let the fun begin! Suitably sparkly and eye-catching clothes can be found cheaply at charity shops, especially in retro styles. (You can supply some pictures of pop stars past for inspiration.) With a lick of hair gel, the children can create anything from a modern messed-up look to a slick fifties quiff! Take some posed photos publicity-shot style, and use them to create a club montage.

Percussion free-play

ACTIVITY

Making music

"From karaoke to drumming, make the music you love . . ."

Instructions

There are a number of ways for children to enjoy the making of music, including:

● Playing instruments. The types of instruments played will depend on the experience of the group. Some children or staff may be accomplished musicians, or they may be learning to play an instrument. Musical ability can be shared through the playing of music, and by teaching the basics to others. Learning to play a simple tune on the recorder or keyboard for the first time can be a real thrill.

Many children first play percussion instruments at nursery or pre-school, and most will have played them at school. This doesn't mean that they will have tired of percussion though, so don't dismiss it for older children. Percussion music can be played without special instruments, equipment or musical knowledge, making it accessible for all. Children often enjoy the time and opportunity to explore 'playing' everyday objects such as milk bottles, which sound different when varying levels of water are poured inside. Drumming workshops can be dynamic. See page 104 for further details. Younger children may still enjoy making simple shakers, rainsticks, guitars and tambourines – see the website section on page 78 for details of instructions. Children may also be inspired to form their own junk band.

Link

- Karaoke can be easily arranged. Children's karaoke machines (essentially just stereos with microphones) can be purchased cheaply, and children can sing along to their favourite tracks.
- There is something about the energy and closeness of listening to or participating in making live music that cannot be replicated by listening or singing or playing along to a recording. Do take the opportunity to expose children to live music when possible, by taking them on trips, or inviting visitors to share their musical skills.

Extension Idea

Older children are likely to prefer to sing to special karaoke recordings, which feature a backing track without the lead vocal, for which the lyrics are supplied. Karaoke tapes, CDs, DVDs and videos are available, and may be hired from libraries. Some children hate singing in public, while others love it. Give everyone the opportunity to sing or opt out. Some children may only feel comfortable singing within a group of friends.

Some children love singing in public

You can conclude the theme by bringing several elements of the activities together in a crescendo. For instance, whether they enjoyed being dance divas or karaoke kings, the children may like to perform for one another in an informal end-of-theme concert. Some may choose to dress up as pop stars and be introduced by their stage name. Others may like their dance routine filmed, music video style. And no doubt, others will have their own unique ideas.

✓ Good practice

Always obtain parental permission before filming children.

Websites

Visit:

www.bbc.co.uk/children/music/ for online karaoke for younger children, and the facility to make music and simple animated videos

www.youthmusic.org.uk/ for information about Youth Music, an organisation which supports music making and training. Details of funding streams are provided

www.thesoundstation.org.uk/jsp/ devised for teenagers by Youth Music, this site encourages participation in music of all genres. Information about regional music opportunities is provided, covering everything from learning an instrument to becoming an MC

www.kinderart.com/teachers/9instruments.shtml for instructions to make simple instruments

7 Light and dark

Aspects of play

Opposites are interesting to explore. Because light and dark are dramatically linked, many activities explore them both simultaneously.

During this theme children can manufacture intriguing 'tricks of the light'. Our brains try to interpret what our eyes see as they take in the light, drawing on our memory banks. But confusing messages result in surprising optical illusions.

Photography requires both light and darkness, so you may like to incorporate activities from pages 1–13.

Resources to support free play

- Shiny resources that catch the light, e.g. foil, tinsel, unwanted CDs, glitter, prisms and sequins.
- Glow-in-the-dark resources, e.g. crayons, paint, face-paint, fabric, paper, card, craft resources including beads, straws, pipe-cleaners, etc.
- A torch for each child is ideal (you could ask the children to bring one in with them).

✔ Good practice

Adventures in the dark are great fun, as long as common sense rules are followed. Ensure adults can always monitor the whereabouts of children, and that there's sufficient light for moving around safely. Bear in mind that some children feel scared or anxious in the dark – let the children know they can opt out of activities at any point or pair up with peers or adults if they prefer.

Remind the children to protect their eyes by never looking directly into a light source (including the sun). Tell them to take care not to shine light sources into people's faces.

Torchlight tag

"Tag with a difference!"

Equipment
- Torches

Instructions

This game is best played outside after dark, but can be played inside with the lights off if you have plenty of hidey-holes.

1. Equip each player with a torch.
2. Choose a volunteer to be 'it'.
3. 'It' stands in the centre of the playground with their eyes closed and their torch off, counting aloud to 50.
4. All other players turn on their torches and hide. Once hidden, players turn off their torches.
5. When they've counted to 50, 'it' turns on his or her torch and looks for the hiding players. 'It' tags the players by shining the torch on them and shouting 'Tagged!'
6. Once tagged, a player should turn on their torch and shine their light directly up in the air (remaining in their hiding place). The game is over when the correct number of lights are shining up, showing everyone has been found.
7. The last player to be found is 'it' in the next round. In large groups you may have more than one 'it' to speed up the game.

Follow-the-flashlight

"Follow the leader with torches!"

Equipment
- Torches

Instructions

1. Equip the children with torches and have them line up side-by-side across the play space.

2. Select a leader, who stands in front of the row of players.

3. The leader should do a simple routine with their torch, such as a sweeping movement in the air, followed by a flash off then on.

4. Players copy. Anyone who makes a mistake is out.

5. The leader does increasingly difficult routines until one player is left. He or she is the next leader.

Torchlight trails captured on camera

Extension Idea

Older children may like to learn Morse code and experiment with sending messages. See the website section on page 93 for details of the Morse alphabet.

Midday, midnight, twilight

"Tell the time to win the game."

ACTIVITY

Instructions

1. Have the group line up one behind the other in order of height, the shortest child at the front. This is necessary as all the children must be able to see you.

2. Stand facing the line of children, about 2 m away from the child at the front.

3. Tell the group the position they're standing in represents 'midday'.

4. Take a large step to the left and have the line copy you, so you are once again directly in front of them. Label this position 'twilight'.

5. Step back again and have children copy. Ask 'Where are we?' (The answer is 'midday'.)

6. Now repeat, but take a step to the right, labelling the position as 'midnight'.

7. Move through the positions a few times with the children copying, until they can comfortably keep up with you. Each time you move, shout out the name of the position.

8. Now you can start to trick the children! Tell them they must still look at you, but go where you say, not where you go. Occasionally fool the group by saying 'twilight' but moving to 'midnight', etc. After a few practice rounds, children who make the wrong move are out.

9. If the players get very good, the slowest into position can also be out.

Extension Idea

In groups of older children you can play a version of this game with torches in the dark. When in the midday position, torches must be off. In the twilight position, they must be on and pointing to the floor. In the midnight position they must be on and pointing towards the sky.

ACTIVITY

SPICE

Torchlight explorers

"Come nocturnal creature spotting.**"**

Exploring by torchlight can reveal a whole different side to a familiar location, even in your own setting. The children can look (and listen) for nocturnal creatures. For instance, many species of spider prefer to come out at night, and slugs and snails feed in the dark.

ACTIVITY

Shadow tag

"Can you capture your opponents' shadows?**"**

SPICE

Instructions

Play this game on a sunny day.

1. Choose a volunteer to be 'it'.
2. 'It' must chase other players and try to tag them. 'It' can only tag by touching a player's shadow with their own shadow.
3. Once tagged the player joins forces with 'it' and also chases other players, attempting to tag them in the same way.

▶

4. The game continues until everyone is tagged. The last player tagged is 'it' in the next round.

5. Keep a close eye on the game. Children occasionally disagree over whether their shadow has been tagged, since it's not as clear to them as when they're tagged with a touch.

Light and dark deco

ACTIVITY

"Dazzling decorating for daytime and night time."

You can decorate the play space to reflect the theme. Shiny objects that catch the light are ideal – you can make glittering mobiles by suspending junk mail CDs from the ceiling or from tree branches. A large collage made from shiny resources will glitter near a light source. Sun catchers hung from the window send rainbow lights across the room, as do mirror balls suspended from the ceiling.

There are plenty of objects that look great in the dark too, especially outside. Fairy lights are popular, and glow-in-the-dark sticks can be pushed into grass and flower pots. Glow-in-the dark beads look fantastic hung from trees. 'Fence tapestry' (see page 86) is an ideal way for settings with wire fencing to decorate their boundaries.

Once decked, you'll have the perfect venue for a glow-in-the-dark disco. You may consider hiring disco lights, and for older children, a black-light. Disco-goers are likely to enjoy the opportunity to wear glow-in-the-dark face-paint (see page 31).

It's fun to pull faces by low lamplight!

Fence tapestry

"Help make a giant tapestry
that glows in the dark!**"**

Equipment
- Glow-in-the-dark fabric remnants
- Glow-in-the-dark ribbon/cord
- Scissors

Instructions

1. Collect a range of glow-in-the-dark fabric remnants in various colours. This may include net, fur fabric, etc. Also collect ribbon, florist ribbon and cord.

2. Cut the fabric into strips approximately 4 cm wide.

3. It's easiest to work with longer strips of fabric, so knot together any short strips to make lengths of at least a metre. Use a double knot to join them securely. Mixing and matching colours and textures adds to the effect.

4. Take a strip of fabric and use a double knot to tie it to the fence. Now weave the fabric alternatively in and out of the holes in the fence. When the strip is coming to an end, tie on another strip with a double knot and continue.

5. You can create a random, decorative pattern in one area of the fence. Or, you can weave a band of tapestry right around the fence to create a glowing perimeter, which has the added benefit of clearly marking the boundaries.

Mini kaleidoscope craft

"Create colourful miniature
patterns in your own kaleidoscope.**"**

Equipment
- Clear camera film canister
- Mirrored card
- Ruler
- Pencil
- Scissors
- Acetate sheet
- Sticky-tape

- Decorative items (see below)
- Electric drill with 5–6 mm bit

Instructions

Kaleidoscope means 'beautiful to see'.

1. Make an eye-hole in the centre of the bottom of the canister with the drill. An electric drill should leave smooth edges.
2. Cut a piece of mirrored card (available from craft suppliers) to size. It must measure 4.5×7.5 cm.
3. Make three folds in the card to form a 3D triangle. The mirrored surface must face inwards. Secure with sticky-tape.
4. Place the triangle in the canister.
5. Trace the outline of the canister lid onto acetate. Cut out the acetate disc.
6. Place decorative items inside the canister lid. Tiny beads, sequins and novelty cake sprinkles (such as flower shapes and balls) work well. Seven to ten items generally suffice.
7. Fit the acetate disc over the decorative items. Don't press the disc in too far – it should prevent the items from falling out but they should still move around.
8. Fit the canister onto the lid. Look through the eye-hole and point the end towards the light. Shake the kaleidoscope and twist the lid to view different patterns.
9. The kaleidoscope works as the light inside the mirrored triangle bounces back and forth, creating interesting reflections of the items inside.
10. You can change the items in the kaleidoscope by removing the disc. If the items don't move sufficiently, you may need to remove one or two.

Monkey in a cage

"You won't believe your eyes!"

Equipment

- Plastic drinking straw
- Scissors
- White card
- Felt-tip pens

ACTIVITY

▶

Instructions

1. Cut two 5 cm squares of card.

2. On one square, draw a monkey (or another animal).

3. On the other square, draw a cage slightly larger than the monkey.

4. Cut two 1 cm deep slits into the top end of the straw to make a mount for the pictures.

5. Put the squares back-to-back with the pictures on the outside, and fit them into the straw.

6. Roll the straw quickly between the palms of your hands. It will appear as though the monkey is in the cage! The children can perform this as a magic trick.

7. This works because your brain can't keep up with the speed of the images. We hold an image in our brain for about one tenth of a second, so instead of seeing the pictures separately in succession, the brain puts the pictures together.

Beheaded!

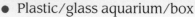

" Amaze your friends with this cool light trick! **"**

Equipment

ACTIVITY

S P I C E

- Plastic/glass aquarium/box
- Water
- Play figure
- Sticky-tack
- Chalk

Instructions

1. Use sticky-tack to stand a toy figure in the bottom of an aquarium.

2. Pour in water until it reaches the neck of the figure.

3. When you look at the figure front on, it will appear normal. Now stand at the side of the aquarium. When you look from a certain angle it will appear as though the figure's head is next to its body, instead of on top of it!

4. Mark the spot on which to stand to see the beheaded figure with a chalk X.

5. Tell a friend to stand in front of the aquarium. Tell him by the time he walks to the chalk X, you'll have magically beheaded the figure.

6. This trick works because from the side you see refracted light coming from under the water, causing an optical illusion.

Catching rainbows

ACTIVITY

SPICE

" Trace a rainbow in this unusual art activity. "

Equipment
- Glass
- Water
- White paper
- Pencil
- Paint

Instructions
When sunlight is streaming through a window ...

1. Place a full glass of water on the window sill.

2. Spread a large sheet of white paper on a table, positioned under the window sill.

3. Slide the glass along the window sill until you catch the light at the necessary angle to produce a rainbow on the paper. If the sunlight is strong and no rainbow is seen, try altering the height of the paper – it may be too close to the glass or too far away.

4. The children can now trace a rainbow, and experiment with mixing paints to create just the right colours to match those shown on the paper.

5. This activity works because the glass of water acts as a prism, splitting the light to create a spectrum. All the colours come from the white light of the sun.

Chromatography craft

ACTIVITY

SPICE

" Find out what colours are made of. "

Equipment
- Blotting paper
- Felt-tip pens
- Saucer of water

Instructions
1. Cut some blotting paper into strips.

2. Draw a thick line with a felt-tip 2 cm from the end of each strip, using a different colour for each strip.

3. Place the strips over the edge of a saucer in turn, with the end below the felt-tip line just dipping into the water.

4. The pigments in each colour will spread up to the top of the strip. They separate because the pigments travel at different speeds. This makes a pretty airbrushed-like effect. The paper can be dried out and used as a craft resource for collages, paper weaving, etc.

ACTIVITY

S P I C E

Shadow puppets

"Puppet fun for everyone!"

Equipment
- Drinking straws
- Card
- Templates (see below)
- Split-pins
- Sticky-tape
- White sheet
- Bright lamp/projector
- Table

Instructions

1. The audience will look at the outline of shadow puppets, not their features, so the shapes should be easily recognisable. Biscuits cutters in various animal and people shapes make good templates. Trace around them onto card and cut the shapes out.

2. Stick the puppets to drinking straws.

3. Hang a sheet from the ceiling. Position a table behind the bottom of the sheet for puppeteers to duck behind.

4. Set up a bright lamp or a projector behind the sheet and turn off the room lights. You're ready for a puppet show!

5. To make more complex puppets, cut the figure's head out separately from the body. Use a split pin to attach the head to the body.

6. Attach another straw to the head. The children can now move the head independently to the body, using both hands to operate the puppet. You can experiment with this principle, making arms move, etc.

Extension Idea

Older children can make sophisticated puppets more faithful to the traditional Chinese shadow puppets. Making and performing with these intricate puppets is a well respected art. See the website section for details of how to make puppets and a shadow puppet theatre complete with a backlit screen.

Children can also make shadow puppets with their hands. However, it's not as easy as it seems! See the website section on page 93 for details of a print out containing pictorial instructions.

ACTIVITY

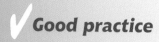

Mirror challenge

"Can you make torchlight bounce?"

Equipment
- Hand-held mirrors/mirror cards
- Torch

Instructions

1. Have the children spread out around the room, equipped with a mirror each.
2. Shine the torch at one mirror. The child holding the mirror must try to angle it to send the beam of light to another mirror.
3. Continue – players must try to bounce the light off as many mirrors as possible. Players can move around the room during the challenge.

✓ Good practice

The children should not hold their mirrors in front of their faces.

Blindfold forfeits

"These fun forfeits will make you laugh!"

Equipment
- Stereo and music
- Paper and pen
- 'Hat' (see below)

Instructions

1. Prepare some forfeits for the children to attempt either blindfolded or with their eyes closed. These might include tying shoe laces, eating yoghurt, writing their name, etc. Write forfeits on slips of paper and place 'in the hat'.
2. Prepare additional resources required, i.e. yoghurt and spoon.
3. Play a game of musical bumps. When a player is out they must pick a forfeit from the hat to perform.

Story dens

"Build your own den and play inside."

Equipment
See instructions below. Optional equipment includes:
- Sheets/blankets, etc.
- Poles/cardboard tubes
- Cord
- Furniture
- Tent
- Torches
- Recorded stories/dramas

Instructions

1. There are several ways of creating simple dens. The children can simply push some tables together and throw a couple of blankets over them. Or, three tall cardboard tubes or wooden poles can be tied at the top with cord to create a tepee frame, over which a sheet is draped. Alternatively, pop-up tents can be erected.

2. Dens and tents create a cosy, darkened atmosphere, perfect for storytelling by torchlight. Tell stories from memory, or play recorded stories (borrowed from the library). Radio plays also work brilliantly in this atmosphere.

Extension Idea

Older children are likely to enjoy storytelling, singing and games around a campfire. See the website section below for information on safely setting and managing a campfire.

Websites

Visit:

- **www.haha.nu/creative/how-to-make-shadows-on-the-wall/** to download pictorial hand shadow instructions
- **www.osv.org/kids/crafts2.htm** for details of making a shadow puppet theatre with older children
- **www.familyfun.go.com/arts-and-crafts/sew/feature/ famf19puppet/famf19puppet5.html** for details of a simple shadow puppet theatre for younger children
- **www.babbage.demon.co.uk/morseabc.html** for the Morse code alphabet
- **www.campingexpert.co.uk/BuildingCampfire.cfm** for advice on campfire safety and activities

8 *Friendship and teamwork*

Aspects of play

This theme celebrates and values friendship and promotes having fun within teams.

Teamwork activities are both fun and challenging. They require children to cooperate and collaborate to achieve a common goal. Children experience leading and following and learn skills they can draw on in real-life situations. Team activities provide opportunities to experience team spirit and feelings of belonging and pride.

Resources to support free play

- Parachute
- Sports equipment
- Craft resources
- Board games, etc.

✓ Good practice

It's important that children feel comfortable within the group before embarking on teamwork activities. If children are new or haven't seen one another for a while (often the case at holiday clubs), begin with some ice-breakers, including a name game – see the suggestions on pages 28 and 67. 'Parachute swap' (see the page opposite) is a popular ice-breaker that explores the commonalities between children.

Parachute swap

"Discover what we have in common."

Equipment:
- Parachute

Instructions

1. Spread the parachute out on the floor.
2. Have the children form a circle around the parachute, then pick it up. Start to 'mushroom' the parachute in unison.
3. The aim is to identify children who have things in common. They must then run underneath the parachute (when it's in the air) to swap places. Call out a few categories in turn, i.e. 'Anyone wearing black socks, change places!' or 'Anyone who had toast for breakfast ...'
4. Now the children have warmed up, ask them to shout out something about themselves in turn which becomes the criteria for swapping places, i.e. 'I like to roller-blade.'

Kangaroo conga

"It's a conga line, but not as you know it!"

Instructions

1. Have the group line up one behind the other. All players hold on to the waist of the child in front, with the exception of the player at the head of the line.
2. The player at the head of the line should call out, 'One, two, three!' On 'three' everyone should jump forward together, attempting to keep the line intact. There will be some hilarity as the first couple of attempts go wrong! When the group gets the hang of it, move on to step 3.
3. Practise until the line can successfully hop to the left and the right.

4. Practise stepping backwards in unison.

5. The player at the head of the line can now shout out random instructions for the group to comply with, i.e. 'One, two, three, back! One, two, three, left!'

Link

6. The children can add their own moves into the mix – turning around for instance so the line is reversed, or adding a Mexican wave (see page 141). They can even develop a conga line routine to music.

Extension Idea

Once they can step back in unison, older children can attempt the trickier manoeuvre of jumping backwards. This move isn't suited to groups with a broad age range as younger children tend to respond more slowly and are liable to be knocked over.

Walking the plank

ACTIVITY

❝Trust your friend to guide you across the plank.❞

SPICE

Equipment:
- Blindfolds
- Chalk

Instructions

1. Have the children form pairs and decide who will be the 'follower' and who will be the 'guide'. Each follower chooses whether to wear a blindfold or to close their eyes.

2. The guide takes the follower's arm and leads them carefully around the room.

3. After a circuit or two, they should lead the follower around by the hand.

4. Once trust has been established, the follower should be comfortable with being led just by the guide's fingertips on their own upturned palms.

5. Now head outside and draw a large boat and shoreline on the playground floor, linked by a gangplank.

6. The followers should take turns to stand at the far end of the boat. Using just their voices and the directions 'forward, back, left and right' the guides should attempt to lead their followers across the gangplank and onto the shore. Each follower has three lives. Lives are lost if the follower 'falls' off the boat or gangplank into the 'sea'.

✔ Good practice

Always allow children to opt out of wearing blindfolds. They can bring up trust issues and feelings of fear for some children.

Extension Idea

Older children can play a more sophisticated trust game based on the same principle:

1. Place obstacles such as chairs around the room.

2. The children form pairs. One wears a blindfold while the other leads them from one side of the room to the other, avoiding the obstacles. This is done by fingertip, and eventually just with directions.

3. To make the game more difficult, fill a few carrier-bags with scrunched up newspaper. Tie a long length of string to the handles of each bag. Tack the other end of the string to the ceiling. The children must now avoid obstacles in the air as well as on the floor.

4. This game can be used as a vehicle to talk about issues around peer pressure. Some groups may like to write peer pressure labels and stick them to obstacles as representation of things they see as potential obstacles/things to avoid in their lives, i.e. smoking, drugs, etc.

Chocolate race

ACTIVITY

SPICE

"This fun game is as delicious as it sounds!"

Equipment
- Dressing-up clothes
- Large bar of chocolate
- Table
- Knives and forks
- Dice

Instructions

This activity requires the children to give and take and respond in good humour when their attempt to eat some chocolate is foiled by another player.

1. Place the bar of wrapped chocolate on the table, along with a knife and fork. In front of the table, place some dressing-up clothes on the floor. This must include gloves as they are intrinsic to the game.

2. Have the children sit in a horseshoe, facing the table.

3. Working clockwise and starting with the child nearest the table, each player should attempt to throw a six in turn. If the first player fails to throw a six, they pass the dice to the person on their left, and so on.

4. When a player throws a six they must call 'Six!' and race to put the clothes on. Only then can they attempt to unwrap and cut off a square of chocolate, using only the knife and fork.

5. Once a player has carved off a square of chocolate they must put down the cutlery and pop it into their mouth with their hand (for hygiene reasons). They must not resume carving until they have finished the chocolate in their mouth.

6. Meanwhile, the remaining players should continue to pass the dice around. When another player calls 'Six!', the current player's turn is over. They must immediately take off the clothes and pass them on. Sometimes the current player won't have managed to get any chocolate, which is part of the game – they have to be quick! It's a good idea to have some extra chocolate to share out at the end of the game if some players haven't faired well.

7. To speed the game up and in large groups you can introduce more than one dice.

If there's a member of the group who can't have chocolate, use an alternative. Apples are equally hard to manage with a knife and fork!

Extension Idea

For older children, a hat, scarf and gloves suffice as a costume. To make the game more difficult, refrigerate the chocolate beforehand and use plastic cutlery!

Sticky buds

"*You'll never be stuck for a friend in this game!*"

ACTIVITY

Instructions

1. Play some music while the children dance around the room.

2. When the music is stopped, the children must join up with a 'bud' (buddy or friend). The 'buds' must 'stick' their body parts together according to your instructions. For instance, if you call 'Sticky-bud heads!', the children must quickly pair up with someone and put their heads together. They must stay like this until the music restarts. You can also ask children to sticky-bud sides of their body, i.e. 'Sticky-bud right hands!'

3. To add a complication, try asking the children to match opposite sides of their bodies, i.e. 'Sticky-bud right foot to left foot.' This introduces some negotiation.

4. For a further complication, have the children sticky-bud in small groups rather than twos, i.e. 'Sticky-bud elbows in threes!'

▶

5. The last players to sort themselves into position and/or players who sticky-bud the wrong body parts can be out (optional).

Extension Idea

Friends often have particular games or pastimes they frequently do together, something they feel is their 'special thing'. You may like to focus on these, and invite friends to share them with the group. For instance, one pair of friends may play a particular clapping game together; another group may devise dance routines to their favourite songs ...

Clapping games require teamwork

Flip it!

"Will your team work together to win the flipping race?!"

Equipment
- Large blanket/tarpaulin

Instructions

1. The blanket/tarpaulin should be just about big enough for everyone to fit both feet on if they squash up closely. Fold it to the right size and place on the floor.
2. Have everyone get on.
3. Challenge the group to completely flip the blanket over, without anyone stepping off onto the floor. This may take up to 15 minutes, depending on the size of the group.
4. Large groups can be split into two teams which can race one another to flip the blanket.

Team identity

"Make yours a dream team!"

On occasion you may divide the children into teams that are intended to work together on a specific project over a period of time. You can encourage individual children to develop a sense of belonging and team spirit by helping to establish team identities. This activity is best suited to children aged over 8 years.

Equipment
- Note paper and pens
- Card
- Felt-tip pens
- Blank stickers/badges (optional)

▶

Instructions

1. Ask each team to talk together to find out what they have in common. Teams should make a note of each commonality, and aim to find as many as possible. (Every member of the team must share the commonalities.) You may like to set a minimum limit, i.e. teams must keep talking until they have 20 entries on their list. (Bigger teams can be given a smaller limit.) At first the children may find similarities that could probably apply to most of the children in the room, such as living in the same town. But after a while the children generally start to talk more about personal things.

2. Have teams draw up a shortlist featuring their top five favourite things that they have in common. This might include being fans of the same band, etc.

3. Challenge the children to come up with a fun team name that reflects one or more of the commonalities on their top five list.

4. Equip teams with paper and felt-tips. Challenge them to come up with one of the following, inspired by their team name/top five:
   - A team logo
   - A coat of arms.

Link

5. You may like to keep the children in their teams and follow up this activity with the team spirit game 'Dead ants' – see page 104.

Extension Idea

You can extend the principle of belonging to small teams to the setting as a whole. For instance, out-of-school clubs can promote a sense of membership of a club amongst attendees by designing a logo, issuing membership cards or badges and even writing a club song. See page 68 for further details.

Link

Promote a feeling of belonging

Dead ants!

"Test your reactions in this fun team challenge.**"**

S P I C E

Instructions

1. Explain that throughout the day whenever the children hear an adult call 'Dead ants!', everyone must stop what they're doing, lie down on their back on the floor and wave their arms and legs in the air (like flailing ants). Have a practice.

2. Divide the group into three or more teams.

3. Each team must come up with their own unusual funny movement to do, and decide on a call that will signal the move.

4. Have each team demonstrate their move to the group in turn. Remember the call that triggers the move of each group. Shout out each team's call in turn as a practice.

5. At random intervals throughout the day shout out each team's call. Occasionally call 'Dead ants!' to have everyone respond together. Make comments on each team's response, i.e. 'You were quick that time!' At the end of the day you may like to give a small prize to the team that consistently responds the fastest.

Drumming workshop

Equipment
- Drums or alternative (see below)

S P I C E

Instructions

1. Gather together drums and/or any items that can be used for drumming, e.g. old saucepans and wooden spoons, empty water cooler bottles, etc.

2. Play a rhythm of seven or eight beats for the children to copy. Have the group repeat it four times (one after the other without stopping). Then call 'Listen!' The children must stop playing and listen as you drum out a new rhythm, which they then repeat as before.

3. When warmed up, call on each child in turn to drum out a new rhythm for the group to copy four times, e.g. 'Listen to Deepak!'

Link   For further teamwork games, see the relays on page 20.

ACTIVITY

S P I C E

Friendship bracelets

"Make a symbol of friendship for your best friend."

Equipment
- Embroidery or floss yarn in three colours
- Sticky-tape

Instructions

1. Take six lengths of yarn, two of each colour. Keeping the threads of the same colour next to one another, tie the threads together by pulling them into a knot at one end. Make the knot 3 cm from the end of the thread.

2. Tape the knotted end to the edge of a table. This helps the children to keep the threads taut.

3. For the purpose of braiding, the threads of the same colour will be moved together as if they are one. Separate the threads into three strands sorted by colour. You will have a left strand, right strand and middle strand.

4. Plait traditionally until 3 cm from the end of the yarn.

5. Tie a knot to hold the plait. Remove from the table.

6. The bracelet is fastened by tying it to the wrist.

Extension Idea

Older children can follow patterns to make more sophisticated, impressive friendship bracelets. See the website section on page 108 for details of patterns.

Friendship wreath

❝Lend a hand to make a symbol of friendship for our wall.❞

Equipment
- Paint and brushes
- Paper
- Backing paper
- Glue

Instructions

The purpose of this activity is to make a symbol that shows friendships are valued within the setting.

1. Have everyone make a right hand print with paint on paper, and leave to dry.
2. Each child cuts out their own handprint.
3. Assemble the hands on a piece of backing paper. Overlap them to make a complete circle. Then glue into position, by applying glue to the heel of the hands. Leave to dry.
4. Bend the fingers back slightly to give a bushy shape.
5. Display on the wall. Alternatively, the wreath can be backed with card, cut out and hung up (as a Christmas wreath would be).
6. When new children start the setting, you can make adding their handprint to the friendship wreath part of the induction programme, explaining its significance.

Collaborative collage

❝Help to make a giant collage – the bigger the better!❞

Equipment
- Chalk/string
- Recycled materials (junk)
- General craft resources
- Additional props (see next page)

Instructions

The aim of this activity is to collaborate to create a giant 3D loose collage (one that isn't stuck in place), using real artefacts, as shown in the photograph below.

1. Mark off a large area of ground/floor that can be dedicated to the collage. Outside this can be done with chalk. If working inside, use string.

2. Get the group together to decide on a scene to depict, i.e. children playing tennis. It's best to stick to simple, bold images.

3. Now consider the resources available and agree how each part of the collage will be created. Think about texture and colour, and about the real objects that can be used, e.g. to create people you might lay T-shirts and shorts on the ground, then draw in heads and limbs with chalk. Alternatively, you could paint the extra features on paper and cut them out (see the example photograph below). Real tennis racquets and balls could be used. White fabric could represent the net, etc.

4. Give the children plenty of time to assemble their collage.

A life-sized collage

Consequences

Link

It can sometimes be very difficult for children to deal with conflict in their friendships. The consequences game can be used to address these issues. It's fully described on page 37, but essentially you need to write scenarios of difficulties in friendships which the children explore through role-play. Also see the website section below.

Websites

Visit:

www.makingfriends.com/friendship.htm for friendship bracelet patterns

www.pbskids.org/itsmylife/friends/friendsfight/index.html this American site has a children's guide on what to do when you fall out with a friend. It includes stories that promote positive conflict resolution techniques

www.gameskidsplay.net/games/ClappingRythmsGames/index. htm for clapping games for two or more players

www.wilderdom.com/games/InitiativeGames.html for team and cooperative game ideas

9 The media

Aspects of play

This theme explores the media in terms of publications, television, radio and animation. It also touches on new media such as podcasting and the internet. This links with the 'Photography and film' theme on pages 1–13, and the 'Drama' theme on pages 27–40. You may like to incorporate activities from these themes.

Resources to support free play

- Magazines
- Newspapers
- Comics
- Notepads
- Pens
- Word processor
- Video camera
- Tape recorder
- Internet access
- Related non-fiction books

✓ Good practice

Remember to get written permission from parents and carers before children are photographed, filmed or recorded. Ensure you have the appropriate licences in place before using media (such as TV) in the setting.

Creating a magazine

"Help to create a magazine. There's a job for everyone!"

ACTIVITY

Equipment
- Children's magazines
- Large sheet of paper
- Felt-tip pens

Instructions

This activity can be completed over the course of several sessions if required.

1. Make available a range of magazines suitable for the age group. Give the children the opportunity to look through them. (You could encourage them to bring in magazines, but not everyone may have access to them.)

2. Gather around a large sheet of paper. Discuss and list the features of magazines that the children enjoy and would like to include in their own version. The following are likely to be mentioned: cartoon strips, puzzles, stories, jokes, competitions, pictures, reviews of music, TV, films and games, problem pages and profiles of famous people. The group may also have some original feature ideas – how about news of your upcoming themes for instance, or a review of your last one?

3. Divide the children into small groups to produce different types of 'copy' for the magazine. (See pages 116–121 for information about drawing cartoons and pages 1-10 for photography ideas – remember you'll need an image for the cover.)

Link

4. Text can be word-processed or hand-written. Once copy has been generated, it must be laid out on the page. Choose a method to suit your resources – work can be reduced in size on a photocopier, then cut out and pasted onto A4 pages in the desired layout. The pasted pages can then be photocopied, collated and stapled. Alternatively, a computer, scanner and printer can be used. The same methods can be used to include children's photographs or artwork.

5. Make a copy of the magazine for each child to take home.

6. It's only practical for most settings to make a magazine as an occasional special project. However, printing newsletters to which the children contribute is simpler. Why not produce a children's newsletter monthly, or at the end of each school holiday?

Extension Idea

Older children may like to include journalistic style articles or columns on subjects that interest or concern them.

CBBC runs a fantastic 'Press Pack' website dedicated to older children interested in journalism. Becoming a member is free, and all members are assigned an editor to work with. Following the many tips and inspiring suggestions on getting and researching a story, telling a story in words and pictures and checking the finished piece, children can write their own reports and submit them to their editor. Reports may be featured on the website, or on children's radio. Each time they take part in activities or submit work, children earn membership points, which eventually gain them access to an additional level of the site. There's even the opportunity to be selected as a guest editor on the children's news programme, *Newsround*. See the website section on page 121 for further details.

Dear editor ...

" *Your contribution could be published in your favourite magazine!* **"**

ACTIVITY

Equipment
- Magazines
- Paper and pens
- Envelopes and stamps

Instructions

1. Make available a range of children's magazines containing contributions from readers. This typically includes:

   - letters to the editor that comment on an article that appeared in a previous edition of the magazine
   - letters that tell a brief, funny story
   - candid photographs
   - jokes.

   A few magazines accept reader's poems and short stories.

   ▶

2. Can the children think of a contribution they could send in for consideration by the editor? Encourage them to assess the tone and length of the pieces included in the magazine, and how they can make their contributions fit in. Check the submission details in the magazine – they may ask for digital photos of a specified size to be sent via email, for example.

3. When the children are ready, they compile their submission. Letters are likely to need a couple of drafts. Encourage the children to keep them brief and to the point.

4. Make a copy of the submission for the children to keep before sending it off via post or email.

5. Magazines print contributions without notification, so keep an eye on new editions.

✔ Good practice

The amount of support children need to compile and send off a submission will vary greatly, so be on hand to help out as required.

Obtain parental permission to submit children's work, and to include the child's name and address if necessary. (Most magazines require, but do not print, addresses.)

Make a range of media available

News magazine programmes

"Be a 'TV' journalist for a day..."

ACTIVITY

SPICE

Equipment
- Notepads and pens
- Newspapers
- Scissors
- Video camera
- Felt-tip pens
- Large pieces of paper
- Sticky-tack
- Local map
- Costumes (optional)

Instructions

This activity is suitable for children aged 8 and over. The younger the children, the more close adult support will be needed.

1. Choose a TV programme format with which the group is familiar enough to make their own version. For our example, we'll take a regional TV news magazine show, the kind typically shown at around 6 p.m. on BBC1 or ITV1.

2. Discuss and list the features of the show:

   a) *Who is on screen?* In our example there are two 'anchors' (presenters), a weather person and a few outside reporters who record reports on location.

   b) *What happens?* The anchors give the main news headlines then read the regional news. Next is the weather forecast. A weather-related picture sent in by a child viewer is shown. Then a couple of regional news items are expanded on by reporters on location – local people connected to the story might be interviewed. The anchors talk to the reporters via an earpiece. There is a 'feel good story' delivered by the anchors – something about an animal perhaps. There is one last round-up of the 'top stories', then the credits roll.

   c) *What does the set look like?* There's a backdrop with the name of the show and a logo. The anchors sit at a desk to read the news. After the weather they sit in chairs with a coffee table between them. The backdrop is the same. The weatherman stands in front of a weather map.

▶

3. Apart from casting the roles, decide what preparation work needs to be carried out behind the scenes in order to make your own show. This is likely to include:
   - making a weather map
   - making backdrops
   - coming up with news stories in the following categories – national headlines, local news, feel good story.

   Split the group into working parties to do the preparation. The children can choose which jobs they'd like to undertake.

4. Equip the children making a backdrop and weather map with large sheets of paper, pencils, felt-tips and any additional craft resources. Those making a map will need access to a real map for reference. Once finished, these prop hands can mount their work on the walls and put together furniture to create an appropriate set.

5. Equip the children who've decided to be journalists with a stack of local newspapers. Have the children trawl through them to look for news stories they might want to feature in their programme. (National headlines are usually included 'in brief' on the second page of local papers.) The children can cut these out.

6. Budding journalists can meet to vote on which stories will be covered. They should also decide which local stories will be developed by the 'reporters on location'.

7. The stories can now be written out as scripts for the anchors/reporters.

8. Cast the on-screen parts and the behind-screen jobs that remain, such as camera operators.

9. Rehearse as necessary, then film the programme. You can make it seem as though the anchors are really cutting live to the reporters on location, without editing. Simply film the programme in the sequence, i.e. film the anchor saying, 'We can now talk to Katie, who's live at the scene for us. What's happening there, Katie?' Then cut, and go outside to film Katie. She can end her report with a link back to studio, etc.

Link

10. You may like to end by rolling credits – see 'Roll the credits' on page 11.

Extension Idea

You may be able to arrange for older children to interview the actual local people involved in current news. They may be able to get a quote to include in their report, or even an interview on camera. In the play setting it's best to stick to interviewing people involved with non-controversial, 'feel good' stories to share.

Older children also enjoy producing a parody or sketch of familiar TV moments, such as a local weather report. For instance, they may do a report just for your town instead of the region, reporting drastically different weather conditions from street to street.

Radio and podcasting

"Create your own broadcast for your friends.**"**

Using audio recording equipment such as a tape recorder or dictaphone, the children can create their own mock radio shows or podcasts for their friends to listen to. A good way to offer this activity is to make the equipment available to the children as part of their free play. You can set up a mock recording studio in a quiet room, manned by an adult. The children can then practise their broadcast or podcast in the main play space, and come to the studio when they're ready to record their piece. The recordings can be played back to the group later, perhaps over lunch or snack time.

You can also offer the opportunity to listen to the radio or podcasts. BBC 7 features children's radio in its programming – see the website section on page 121 for further details.

Visits and visitors

You can arrange for your group to visit a real TV or radio studio. Most local studios (and all BBC ones) have public open days periodically, and many will arrange for someone to show a group of visitors around in between times too. Alternatively, you can invite a DJ or presenter from your TV or radio station to visit the group and talk about their jobs. (They often have plenty of station merchandise such pens and stickers to give away too.)

A local radio station may even be interested in coming to record a brief interview with you and one or two children about the media theme, which could air locally.

Creating a mock radio show

Animation antics

"Make your own animated art and cool cartoons!"

ACTIVITY

There are three categories of animation.

Stop start animation
As used in *Wallace and Gromit*, clay characters are posed, filmed briefly, then painstakingly moved a little, and filmed in the new position.

It's a very slow process, but with just a video camera and Plasticine, older children can try out the technique. Younger children can simply design and create a cartoon character from clay, and try out different poses. When finished, the clay can be left to harden, then painted and varnished for posterity.

2D animation

This is the original animation technique, as used in *The Simpsons*. Each frame of action is painted then filmed. This technique relies on cartoon artists.

There are many books and websites that teach how to draw cartoons. See page 121 for details.

Computer generated animation (CGI)

This is used in *Finding Nemo*, for example, and for special effects in live, non-animated films. Digital computers and 3D software are used.

Mastering CGI takes a lot of time and the right equipment. However, children can visit the online Flux Studio (see the website section) to learn the basics of designing and recording clips of CGI animation. Younger children will be able to achieve one or two quick results. Older children can progress to produce more sophisticated clips, even uploading and animating their own clip art.

Extension Idea

Older children can work as professional animators do and start off by devising a plan of their story, known as a 'storyboard'. The animator writes down the 'key frames' that are needed to tell the story, and the sequence they will appear in. He or she then works on the 'tweening' – the process of working out what frames are needed in between the key frames in order to link them together. The frames are then sketched out one after another, cartoon-style, on a large board. This is referred to throughout the animation process.

Thaumatropes

"Make an animated spinning disk to amaze your friends!"

Equipment

- Card
- Ruler
- Pencil
- Felt-tip pens
- Hole punch
- 2 elastic bands

Instructions

Loosely translated from Greek, 'thaumatrope' means 'magic turning'.

1. Cut two card rectangles measuring 7 cm × 12 cm.
2. The rectangles will be used in the landscape position. Use a ruler to find the middle of one rectangle, and mark the point with a pencil dot.
3. Now divide the rectangle in half by drawing a faint pencil line across it. (The line will pass through the central dot.)
4. Use the hole punch to make one hole at each end of the rectangle, at the halfway point – see the diagram on page 119.
5. Draw a simple owl in the middle of the card. The wings should be pointing downwards. Go over the pencil lines with a felt-tip for a bold image.
6. Repeat steps 2–4 with the second card rectangle.
7. Place the second rectangle over the first, lining up the holes. Hold the cards against a window, and trace the body of the owl onto the second rectangle. Don't trace the wings.
8. Draw in spread wings (as they would appear in flight).
9. Now turn the second card upside down, and place it back-to-back with the first, lining up the holes.
10. Thread an elastic band halfway through the holes in one end of the rectangles (so there is an elastic loop extending on both sides). Take one loop, thread it through the other and pull tight against the card, creating a half-hitch knot.
11. Repeat on the opposite end of the rectangle.
12. To spin the thaumatrope, pull the bands taught. The owl will appear to flap its wings.

13. The children can now experiment with the method, i.e. by writing their first name on one card and second name on the other, or by drawing an animal on one card and its habitat on the other. The children can also make circles or squares instead of rectangles. In the case of squares, punch the holes at opposite corners for a good spin.

Link

Also see 'Monkey in a cage' on page 87.

Punch a hole at each end of the rectangle.

Thaumatropes

Flip books

" *Design your own animated book.* **"**

Equipment
- Notebook
- Pencil
- Felt-tip pens

ACTIVITY

Instructions

1. Decide on a simple picture to animate, such as a rocket taking off.

2. Starting on the back page of the notebook, draw a rocket in the air. The picture should be drawn on the outside edge of the paper, towards the top.

▶

3. Now turn to the penultimate page. Draw the rocket again, this time slightly lower down on the page. Starting at the back of the book enables you to refer to the previous image easily.

4. Continue drawing the rocket in a slightly different position on each page, until the rocket is in the launch position. (It doesn't matter if this isn't at the very front of the notebook).

5. Hold the notebook by the spine in your left hand. Use your right hand to bend the book slightly with your thumb on the front page. Allow the pages to flip quickly past your thumb. The rocket will be animated – it will appear to fly.

6. Try out other designs.

Extension Idea

Flip books are for all ages – there are even competitions for adults. Older children can make more sophisticated books designed to tell a simple story rather than to animate a single image. These work well with a humorous twist. For instance, a man might walk into a lamppost, then fall down and see stars in typical cartoon-style.

Website design

Older children may be interested in helping you to set up/maintain a website for your setting. Members' pages can include theme reviews and future activity plans, and are a great way to involve children in the running of the setting. Younger children can help to create an online gallery featuring pictures of their artwork. See the website section on page 121 for details of advice on designing your site.

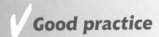

✔ Good practice

When using the internet with children, their safety is paramount. Never allow children to reveal any personal details. Always follow your setting's good practice guidelines and policies.

Exploring the world wide web

Websites

Visit:

www.bbc.co.uk/cbbc/presspack/index.shtml for older children interested in the news and reporting

www.bbc.co.uk/bbc7/bigtoe/ for details of BBC children's radio

www.fluxtime.com/animate.php to create animation in the Flux Studio

www.bbc.co.uk/bbcfour/documentaries/features/ animation-nation.shtml for animation clips and information

www.unclefred.com/ and **www.artistshelpingchildren.org/ howtodraw.html** to learn to draw cartoons

www.mangatutorials.com/ to learn to draw Manga-style cartoons; suitable for older children

www.build-your-website.co.uk/index.htm for advice on setting up a website from scratch

10 Space

Aspects of play

This theme draws on the reality of astronomy, space and space travel as well as the fantastical realm of science fiction, inhabited by aliens aplenty! In the play setting, reality and fantasy can be explored together.

You can supplement the activities with intriguing information about space. For instance, you can tell children about the 1960s Soviet/American space race to moon walk when introducing the 'Space race game' (page 124). Children can find out about constellations when making 'Stargazer scopes' (page 126).

Resources to support free play

- Non-fiction and fiction books
- Internet access
- Space small world toys such as spacecrafts, astronaut and alien figures, etc.

Alien grass heads

""Make an out-of-this-world alien and watch his green hair grow!""

Equipment
- Tights/stockings
- Sawdust
- Grass seed
- Coloured elastic bands
- Yoghurt pots
- Coloured paper
- Scissors
- Glue stick
- Decorative craft resources (see below)

Instructions

1. Cut the foot section from a pair of tights or a stocking.

2. Place a small handful of grass seed into the toe section. This will be the top of the alien's head. When the grass grows, the alien will have green 'hair'.

3. Top up with sawdust to fill out the foot. Aim to make the alien head about the size of a large potato.

4. Tie a secure knot in the opening. Cut off any excess stocking.

5. Mould into an oval head shape. You'll find the sawdust is easy to manipulate.

6. To create features such as eyes and noses (perhaps several of each!) and weird alien lumps and bumps, pinch out a small section of sawdust filled stocking and twist tightly. Wrap a colourful elastic band around the twist to secure it. Repeat as required.

7. Use general craft resources and glue to decorate – the more colourful and shiny the better. A sprinkling of glitter gives a space-dust effect. Wobbly eyes look great (these can be on stalks if you make the twists as instructed in step 6). Pipe cleaners can be pushed directly into the head – they make good mouths and antennae. You can also colour with felt-tips directly onto the stocking. Avoid putting glue on the toe section where the grass will grow. Leave to dry.

8. Cover a yoghurt pot with paper and decorate. If desired, you can make the pot look like the alien's body by wrapping around pipe-cleaner arms and adding paper feet to the bottom of the pot.

▶

9. Sit the head in the pot and place on a windowsill in a warm room. Water little and often with care not to ruin the decoration. The sawdust should feel damp (not soaked) afterwards.

10. The children can watch the 'hair' grow, and style it with scissors repeatedly!

✔ Good practice

Sawdust can be an allergen for children with respiratory conditions such as asthma or skin conditions such as eczema. You can use compost as a substitute, but it is more difficult to mould and shape. Use sawdust in a well-ventilated room, and as with all dusty substances, encourage children not to breathe it in.

ACTIVITY

S P I C E

Space race game

"Will your team win a prize in our space race?"

Equipment
- Newspapers
- Recycled material (junk)
- Sticky-tape
- Glue sticks
- Scissors
- Decorative items (see below)

Instructions

1. Place in the centre of the room a large collection of recycled materials from which models can be made. This should include boxes, yoghurt pots, plastic bottles, etc. Also make a stack of newspapers available.

2. Split the children into teams of four or five.

3. Explain that the purpose of the activity is for each team to build the best rocket possible from the materials available, within the time limit given.

4. Equip each team with sticky-tape, scissors and a glue stick.

5. On your signal, teams should start making their rocket. It's best to play the timing by ear, but most groups need in the region of 15 minutes.

6. Call a halt to the rocket building and put the recycled materials away. Replace them with a range of decorative craft resources including shiny materials, e.g. foil, unwanted CDs from junk mail, etc. Allow a further period for teams to decorate their rocket.

7. Lastly, give the children a few minutes to think of a name for their rocket. They should also decide on any special features the rocket has – encourage the children to be creative and have some fun with this. For instance, one group may say their rocket has a sunroof, while another might have a heat-seeking alien detector.

8. Together the whole group should go to see each team's rocket in turn. The team in question should introduce it by name and explain its special features.

9. Award titles such as 'Tallest Rocket', 'Most Creative', 'Funniest Features', 'Best Name', etc. You may like to have an overall winner – 'Most Impressive' – and reward the relevant rocket builders with a small prize.

Blast-off!

Extension Idea

Even older children enjoy the space race game. But it's preferable to ask them to incorporate special features in their rocket design from the outset, so they can actually represent them in some way on their model.

Stargazer scopes

ACTIVITY

SPICE

"Create a mini planetarium complete with your own constellations.**"**

Equipment

- Kitchen roll tube
- Black paper
- Pencil
- Sticky-tape
- Large needle
- Non-fiction astronomy book

Instructions

1. Stand the end of the kitchen tube on the black paper. Draw a circle around it.

2. Cut out the circle allowing an extra centimetre all the way around. Cut four slits at regular intervals from the outer edge of the circle into the pencil line, creating four flaps.

3. Place the circle over the end of the cardboard tube. Fold the flaps down and stick them to the side of the tube. If there are any gaps between the paper and the tube, close them with tape to avoid letting in light.

4. Constellations are created by making a few holes in the paper with a needle. The children can copy a constellation such as the Big Dipper from a book, or create their own constellation – they may make their initials for instance. It's a good idea to make the design in pencil dots first, then pierce through them with the needle.

5. Look through the open end of the stargazer scope, and point the other end towards the light to see an impressive mini planetarium effect.

ACTIVITY

SPICE

Space suits

❝*Try on some galactic gear!*❞

Equipment
- Large roll of white paper
- Shiny foil
- Fabric remnants
- Scissors
- Large strong bin bags
- Sticky tape
- Decorative craft supplies
- Pictures of astronauts for inspiration
- Camera (optional)

Instructions

In this activity, the children creatively fashion a space suit with the resources provided. Scrap stores often stock foil, shiny objects and large rolls of paper.

1. Equip the children with a bin bag each and ask them to find a partner. Partners should help each other to fashion space suits throughout the activity.

2. The bin bags make the base of the space suits, and prevent the need to tape additional resources to the children's own clothes. Cut arm and head holes in the bin bags so they can be slipped on. Additional bags can be cut, wrapped around the arms and legs and taped in place.

3. Children are often absorbed enough to spend extended periods of time adding to this base to create a space suit. Remember to provide access to a mirror, and time for the children to play imaginatively in their suit. You may also like to take a photo of each child at the end of the session as the space suits are disposable.

Moon surface

" Create some craters in our moon art project. "

ACTIVITY

When placed on a table, the moon surface can be used as a play base for small-world space play.

SPICE

Equipment
- Stiff card
- Plaster of Paris
- Bubble wrap
- Newspaper
- Black paper
- Sticky-tape
- Paint and brushes
- Pebbles
- Glitter
- Pipe cleaners
- Paper
- Felt-tip pens
- Recycled materials

Instructions

1. Decide how large you would like the moon surface to be, and use an appropriately sized piece of thick card as a base. (An opened out cardboard box would suffice.)

2. Tear a few sheets of newspaper into the desired size, lightly scrunch and use to give the moon surface texture, creating craters, etc. Tape the newspaper into place. A rough finish and abstract shapes are fine.

3. Cut enough bubble wrap to completely cover your base. Smooth it over the newspaper peaks and troughs and tape down. Use as much tape as necessary to make the wrap mimic the shape of the newspaper textures beneath.

4. Make up plaster of Paris according to the instructions. Spread a thin layer over the bubble wrap and leave to dry.

5. Paint as desired and leave to dry.

6. Meanwhile, you can make a backdrop for the wall by painting stars on black paper. You can do this by flicking yellow and white paint onto the paper from the brush. Leave to dry, then mount on the wall.

7. Add a few 'moon rock' pebbles to the surface. The real articles are quite plain, but children can decorate them anyway they like.

8. Twist brightly coloured pipe cleaners into alien figures, and white or silver pipe cleaners into astronauts (representing the colour of space suits). Draw faces on paper, cut them out and stick them to the figures.

9. A space station and rockets can be made from recycled materials (small boxes, etc.) if desired.

Making a backdrop for the wall

Blastoff!

"Make and launch your own flying spacecrafts!"

There are two ways to make and launch spacecrafts outlined below. The first method is best suited to younger children.

Method 1

Equipment
- Paper bags
- Felt-tip pens
- Balloons

Instructions
This is a simple activity, but children love it and will repeat it over and over again.

1. Decorate paper bags to look like a spacecraft, e.g. a rocket or a UFO.
2. Partially blow up a balloon. Hold the end closed instead of tying a knot.
3. Insert the balloon into the bag, and let go. The deflating balloon will launch the spacecraft in the air.

Method 2

Equipment
- Kitchen roll tube
- Camera film canister
- Scissors
- Sticky-tape
- Paper
- Felt-tip pens
- Decorative craft resources
- Water
- Effervescing (fizzing) antacid tablet
- Eye protection (see below)

Instructions

1. Cut a kitchen roll tube in half widthways. You'll need one half per rocket, so keep one section of tube and set the other section aside.
2. Cut a straight line lengthways up the section of tube, as you need to adjust the size to make the tube fit the film canister.
3. Tape one edge of the tube to the canister. Roll the tube tightly around the canister to make the body of the rocket. Tape down securely.
4. To make a nose cone for the rocket, cut a circle from paper. Cut a pie-shaped wedge from the circle. Pull the cut edges together, overlapping them into a cone shape. Secure with tape. You can experiment with different sized cones by varying the size of circle – this affects the flight of the rocket.
5. Decorate the rocket using felt-tips and other craft resources, e.g. star stickers, sequins, etc.
6. You can experiment with adding paper fins if you wish.

To launch the rocket

1. Go outside. Put on eye protection (safety glasses, sunglasses or goggles suffice).
2. Take the lid off the canister. With the rocket upside down, pour water into the canister until a quarter full.
3. Put an antacid tablet in the canister, replace the lid quickly and BACK AWAY!
4. Within a few seconds the rocket will launch into the air. You can experiment with using two tablets.
5. Remember to find and pick up the tablets after every launch. You can sometimes re-use them. If not, dispose of safely.

✔ **Good practice**

Closely supervise the use of the tablets. Make sure the children know not to put them in their mouths, and not to take their hands to their mouths after handling them. Hands must be washed after the activity. Check no one has an allergy to antacid tablets. Also see the good practice advice on using film canisters on page 5.

Link

ACTIVITY

Comet catch

❝*Create a comet ball and play comet catch.*❞

Equipment
- Fabric remnants (see below)
- Rice
- Ribbon
- String
- Scissors

Instructions
Comet balls are so called because of their shape – they have streamers coming from one end which look like the tail of a comet. This makes the balls easier to catch than usual.

To make comet balls

1. Cut a 15 cm square from fabric.
2. Place a quarter cup of rice in the centre.
3. Cut four long lengths of ribbon. Place the end of each length on top of the rice.
4. Twist the fabric into ball, with the ribbon ends on top of the rice caught in, and the rest of the ribbon streaming free.
5. Hold the fabric still while someone else helps out by tying the top tightly with string. Cut off any excess.

To play comet catch

1. Write forfeits on slips of paper and put them in a bag. Include commands such as 'down on one knee', 'one hand behind your back', 'clap your hands twice', and so on. Take the bag outside with you.
2. Everyone stands in a circle. Choose a volunteer to be 'comet chief' – he or she stands in the centre of the circle.
3. The chief throws a comet ball to players at random. They must catch it and throw it back. If a player misses they take a forfeit. They must perform the forfeit successfully before returning to the game normally, i.e. a player must successfully catch the ball while down on one knee before standing up again.
4. When a player has scored three catches in a row, he or she becomes the new chief, swapping places with the previous one.

✔ Good practice

It's a good idea to keep comet balls among your outside resources as children who have difficulty catching balls (perhaps due to a physical impairment) may find it easier to join in with ball games when they are used as a substitute.

Coloured star biscuits

ACTIVITY

S P I C E

"Bake delicious biscuits that are the colour of real stars."

Equipment

- 50 g castor sugar
- 50 g soft butter
- 130 g plain flour
- 1 small egg
- Boiled sweets (see below)
- Star shaped cutter
- Mixing bowl and spoon
- Sieve
- Rolling pin
- Knife
- Spatula
- Lined baking sheet

Instructions

1. Explain that although stars look like twinkling white lights to us, some have a colour tone that reflects how hot the stars are burning. The hottest have a blue tone and the coolest a red tone. The stars somewhere in between have a yellow to orange tone.
2. Pre-heat the oven to 180° or Gas Mark 4, and line a baking sheet with greaseproof paper.
3. Place the butter in the bowl. Sieve and mix in the sugar.
4. Beat in the egg.
5. Sieve and stir in the flour.
6. Kneed the mixture into a ball by hand. Flour a clean surface (e.g. a chopping board) and roll out the mixture to 0.5 cm thick.
7. Cut the mixture into star shapes with the cutter. Use a spatula to lift these onto the baking tray.
8. Use a smaller cutter to cut a hole from the star shapes. If you don't have a small enough cutter, cut out a simple square shape with a knife.
9. Drop a boiled sweet into each hole. Choose oranges, reds, yellows and blues. If you can't find blue sweets, you can always try mixing the colours! If the sweets are too big for the holes, crush them with a rolling pin first.
10. Cook until lightly golden, approximately 12–15 minutes. Leave to cool until the melted boiled sweet turns hard.
11. Peel off the greaseproof paper. The biscuits are now ready to serve.

Extension Idea

Space makes a great topic for a quiz as there are so many interesting facts and figures, and questions can be pitched at different levels to suit the age group with which you work. Older children may enjoy the addition of some science fiction questions. See page 154 for instructions on the 'Noughts and crosses quiz', which can be played with space questions.

Link

Websites

Visit:

www.nasa.gov/audience/forkids/home/index.html for information for older children including details of current space projects, plus activities, art and stories for younger children

www.spaceplace.jpl.nasa.gov/en/kids/svlbi_do1.shtml print out a free black hole board game, worth laminating for durability

www.factmonster.com/quizzes/space/1.html for an online space quiz suitable for older children

www.artyastro.com/main.htm for online space games and activities, including the facility to design a space scene and print it out for colouring or painting

www.amazing-space.stsci.edu/resources/explorations/trading/game.htm a quiz for over 8s that rewards correct answers with space trading cards

11 Sport

Aspects of play

Not everyone enjoys participating in organised sports, and even children who do, need variety and time to rest. So this theme adds a fun twist to sporting pursuits, and includes plenty of complementary, non-sporting activities alongside traditional sports. It celebrates having fun as much as competing and winning.

Good sportsmanship and team spirit are synonymous with sport. You can incorporate activities suggested in the 'Friendship and teamwork' theme – see pages 94–108.

Resources to support free play

- Good range of sports equipment
- Assorted craft resources
- Internet access
- Related fiction and non-fiction books, etc.

Your own Olympic Games

You may like to centre this theme on your own Olympic Games. It doesn't have to be an Olympic year – you can hold your version whenever you like! Consult with the group about the Olympic events they would like to include (see the Consultation chapter, pages 203–207). You can adapt these to suit your own purposes. For instance, perhaps in your Games football will be five-a-side, and the shot-put will be replaced by throwing a rubber ball.

But you needn't stick to replicating real Olympic events, and your definition of 'sport' is up to you! You can include darts, pool and even boomeranging and Frisbee throwing alongside non-physical novelty events such as tournaments of tiddlywinks or hangman. Ensure there's a good range of activities in terms of levels of physicality and skill, and team and individual pursuits.

Olympic training

Your Olympics needn't focus on competing. You can place the emphasis on *training* for the Games. After all, competing in the Olympics is only a brief part of an athlete's career. You can provide opportunities for the children to practise whatever events they wish, rounding off with some competitive events that the children can enter if they choose.

The internet is a great place to research training techniques for particular sports. (Potential footballers may practise ball control by dribbling a ball in and out of cones for instance.) The excellent CBBC site is a good starting point – see the website section on page 147.

> ✔ **Good practice**
>
> Don't initiate training that requires specialist supervision unless you're a qualified coach. However, you could invite a coach to visit the group and run a safe training session. Parental permission for participation will be required.

Olympic spirit

⌃ Link ⌄

You can celebrate the Olympic spirit by holding an opening ceremony, featuring a fancy dress jamboree and the ritual parading of the Olympic torch around the 'stadium' (see below). The children can design flags and even write their own anthems for their teams (see page 68). Alternatively, you could put countries' names 'in the hat' and have teams randomly select the country they'll represent. This brings in opportunities for the children to explore other countries and cultures, which you can always develop further.

Medal ceremonies on makeshift rostrums are fun to role-play. Simple gold, silver and bronze medals can be made from discs of cardboard covered in foil and suspended from ribbon. You may like to add a 'participation medal' to the list, or supplement the medals with rosettes (see page 139).

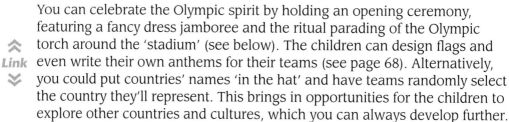

Olympic torch

" Help to make a symbolic torch. "

Equipment

ACTIVITY

- Sugar paper
- Pencil
- Card
- Cellophane and tissue paper in fire colours
- Newspaper
- Elastic band
- Silver paper
- Glue stick
- Stapler

Instructions

This is an imitation of a wooden and metal torch design.

1. Fold a large sheet of brown sugar paper in half. Draw the outline of a torch approximately 60 cm long (essentially a tall cone shape with a rounded bottom).

2. Cut out with the paper still folded to give you a back and a front.

Olympic torch parade

3. Lay one torch shape on the silver paper. Trace the shape of the top third of the torch, then remove from the paper – you've drawn the top of a cone. Finish this off freehand, making the cone no longer than 30 cm in total. Cut the cone out. Line up the top of the silver cone with the top of the torch front and glue into place. (See the picture on page 137.)

4. Staple the back and front together along the edges. Stuff out with a little shredded newspaper.

5. Make a template for the flames that will come from the top of the torch. Draw a flame shape of approximately 30 cm on card and cut it out.

6. Trace this shape onto cellophane and tissue paper in shades of orange, red and yellow and cut them out. You'll need at least nine flames.

7. Gather the flames together in a bunch. Use an elastic band to hold the bottom of the flames together.

8. Sit the bunch of flames in the top of the torch. Use a couple of staples on either side to secure the flames to the torch.

All of the following activities can be combined with your own Olympics, or used as standalone activities.

Cheerleading

"Make pom-poms and learn to cheer."

Equipment
- Shredded coloured paper (see below)
- Elastic bands
- Masking tape

ACTIVITY

SPICE

Instructions

To make pom-poms

1. To make bushy pom-poms, you need a good quantity of shredded paper. You can buy shredded craft paper, but if you have access to a shredder you may find it cheaper to make your own. Choose paper in bold colours and metallics. Keep the shredded paper as flat as possible.

2. Take a few handfuls of shredded paper and straighten it out. Take hold of the ends of the strands and build up a bunch of paper. Keep adding to this until you have a bushy pom-pom shape.

3. Twist an elastic band 5 cm from the bottom of the bunch to hold the shreds together. This also creates a handle. Wrap a couple layers of masking tape around the length of the handle so the paper won't tear when the pom-pom is used.

4. Repeat to make a second pom-pom.

Cheering

The squad should stand in a formation in the starting position – pom-poms on the ground in front of them, standing straight with arms by their sides and fists closed. Cheerleaders can take it in turns to be the captain who stands front and centre, leading cheers. The squad can learn the cheer below, then make up their own. Actions are shown in brackets. After an action is taken, cheerleaders should quickly return to the starting position. When (x) is shown, cheerleaders make an x shape with their arms and legs.

Hello Cheer
[Captain calls] HELLO!
[Squad answers] HELLO!
[All] We're the team that's got the spirit, [clap, clap]
Wherever we go, we like to bring it! [clap, clap]
From coast [x] to coast [x],
We cheer the most [x],
So fans have a nice day –
From our team, now LET'S PLAY! [crouch down, pick up pom-poms, jump up shaking pom-poms and whooping]

✔ **Good practice**

Paper shredders are not suitable for children's use, so shred paper yourself in advance of the session.

Rosettes

❝Show your support with a rosette in your favourite sport team's colours.❞

ACTIVITY

Equipment
- Card
- Cup and saucer
- Pencil
- Scissors
- Felt-tip pens
- Ribbon
- Stapler
- Badge blank/safety pin and stickers

▶

Instructions

This activity is best suited to children over 8 years.

1. Draw around a saucer to make a card circle. Cut it out. Now draw a smaller inner circle by placing the cup upside down in the centre of the circle and drawing around it.

2. The outer circle is where the ribbon will go. Decorate the inner-circle with felt-tips, writing the name of the team supported, etc, using the team colours.

3. Choose ribbon in the appropriate team colours. Cut a length twice as long as the circumference of the rosette. Cut a V shape into each end to prevent fraying.

4. Fold over one end of the ribbon to make a neat edge. Staple it to the outer circle, side on.

5. Now concertina the ribbon (as though making a fan) to create pleats. These need to be angled to accommodate the circular card. Staple each pleat at its base as you work. The next pleat will cover the staple.

6. When you get to the end, cut off any spare ribbon, and cut the end into a V shape. Fold over the end tidily and staple in place.

Medal ceremonies are great fun

7. Now either fix a safety pin to the back of the rosette with stickers (several layers for strength) or glue a badge blank – small blank cardboard badges available from stationers – to the back of the rosette.

8. If you want to award rosettes, write what the award is for in the centre, in place of a team name.

ACTIVITY

Mexican wave game

"It's a celebration wave with a difference!"

Equipment
- Parachute
- Balls

Instructions

The Mexican wave is a celebration cheer done by crowds to show appreciation for their team.

1. Place some chairs side by side in a horizontal row and have the children sit down. Do a couple of Mexican waves as though the group are spectators at a sports event. The child at the end of the line stands up and raises their arms above their head, then in a fluid movement, lowers them and sits down. As soon as the first child is out of their chair, the child next to them starts the same movement, and so the wave spreads down the line. Send the wave straight back by beginning again at the opposite end.

2. Now lay the parachute on the floor. Have the children form a circle around it and pick it up.

3. Whist holding the parachute have the children raise and lower their arms in a wave as before (but this time they stand throughout). This makes the parachute rise and dip as the wave goes round the circle.

4. Drop a lightweight football onto the centre of the parachute and have the children repeat the wave. With good timing the group can send the ball rolling around the edge of the parachute. (The ball may shoot off a few times at first).

5. Once some successful circuits have been achieved, introduce a second ball to the game.

6. You can continue to make the game more challenging as the group improves by adding more and/or smaller balls.

Frisbee

"Learn to play golf and basketball – with a Frisbee!"

ACTIVITY

S P I C E

Equipment
- Frisbees
- Brightly coloured ribbon
- Goals (see below)
- Chalk

Instructions

Golf
This is ideally played over a large area, such as a park.

1. Pick a point to 'tee off' (throw the Frisbee) from. Estimate how far the children can throw. Select a target about 2½ times this distance away as the first 'hole'. This could be a tree, etc. Tie or place the ribbon on the 'hole'.
2. Continue, marking out a course of 9 or 18 holes.
3. The children work their way around the course, counting how many throws it takes them to touch each hole with the Frisbee. Players must throw from the spot where their Frisbee lands each time. The player with the lowest score wins.

Basketball

1. Lay out a court with goals at either end – these can be large or small to suit the group. Clean rubbish bins work well. Draw a chalk baseline in front of each goal.
2. Divide the group into two teams, and decide which will be 'on' first.
3. A player from the 'on' team throws the Frisbee in from their baseline. The object is for the team to score a goal by passing the Frisbee up the court, while the opposing team tries to intercept and score a goal at the opposite end.
4. No guarding of players or goals is allowed. Players must stand still when in possession of the Frisbee.
5. When a goal is scored, the successful player throws in from their own baseline.

Extension Idea

Older children can progress to playing 'Nest' in threes. At any one time two players are 'on' and one is 'out'. An 'on' player 'nests' two Frisbees one on top the other and throws them to their opponent, who attempts to catch both. The catch only counts if the Frisbees separate in the air and are both caught. If this happens, the Frisbees stay in play. The catcher now throws the 'nest' and the game continues. If not, the 'out' player must decide who was most at fault, the thrower or the catcher. He or she swaps places with this player, and is now 'on'.

ACTIVITY

Boomerang

S P I C E

"*Make and throw your own boomerang.*"

Equipment

- Scissors
- 30 cm ruler
- Pencil and eraser
- Felt-tip pens
- Cardboard box

Instructions

To make the boomerang

1. Open out a cardboard box (the sort with corrugated card in the middle, not flat card as in a shoe box).
2. Place the ruler in the centre and trace around it.
3. Turn the ruler perpendicular to the middle of the shape you've traced. Trace the ruler again in this position. (You will have formed a symmetrical cross.)
4. Cut out the boomerang shape. Erase unwanted pencil lines, and decorate with felt-tips.
5. Gently curve the edges up slightly with your hand.

To throw the boomerang

1. Only throw the boomerang outside in an area with clear space.
2. Hold the boomerang straight up with your arm fully extended and the boomerang perpendicular to the floor. The curves should be facing you.
3. Throw the boomerang upwards (not straight out). Let it circle back to you and attempt to catch it!
4. If a child struggles to make their boomerang work, check they're holding it perpendicular to the floor and throwing it upwards – it won't work if thrown outwards on its side like a Frisbee.

ACTIVITY

S P I C E

Kit design

"Make yourself a kit to be proud of!"

Equipment
- Plain T-shirts
- Pencil
- Paper
- Fabric paints

Instructions

1. Either have the children bring in an old, plain T-shirt from home, or supply them (perhaps bought from a charity shop).
2. Make some pictures of sports teams available. What do the children like/dislike about their kits? How would they improve them?
3. Encourage the children to come up with their own design for a sports top. They might like to design an emblem for the front and emblazon their name across the back, etc. They can try out ideas on paper before sketching the design onto their T-shirts.
4. Following the manufacturer's instructions, paint over the design with fabric paints. When dry it's generally necessary to iron items before they become colourfast.

Extension Idea

Older children can focus on sports/leisure wear in terms of fashion items. All they need to get started on designing their own collection for the coming season is a fashion template and some coloured pencils. You can download printable templates online – see the website section on page 147 for details. Deciding on design, colours and accessories involves trial and error, so provide plenty of templates per person.

ACTIVITY

Make a sports soap

"When you've washed enough, you'll have a ball to keep!"

Equipment
- Small high-bounce ball
- Washing-up liquid
- Clean margarine container
- Glycerine soap
- Sharp knife
- Jug
- Microwave

Instructions

1. Wash the ball with washing-up liquid. When dry, place in the container – this will be the soap mould.
2. Cut the soap into dice-sized cubes and place in an old jug. (Warm soap in the microwave for a few seconds if it's too hard to cut easily.)
3. Place the jug of soap in the microwave to melt, *not boil*. Heat for a few seconds at a time, and then check progress.
4. Carefully pour melted soap into the container, covering the ball.
5. Cool. Then set in the fridge.
6. When completely set, twist the container slightly to pop out the soap.

ACTIVITY

Healthy eating

❝Make some delicious, healthy treats.❞

Equipment

To make 16 cereal bars:

- 1½ cups plain flour
- ¾ cup of sugar substitute
- 1 egg
- 1 tsp cinnamon (optional)
- 1 tsp baking powder
- ½ cup dried fruit
- 1 cup apple sauce
- 2 cups Cheerios cereal
- Non-stick healthy cooking spray
- 2 mixing bowls and spoons
- Sieve
- Sharp knife
- Baking sheet approximately 30 × 20 cm
- Cooling rack

Instructions

1. Sieve the flour into a bowl. Stir in the baking powder, cinnamon and the dried fruit of your choice – dried cherries and cranberries work well. You can buy both in 'bits' which saves chopping.
2. Beat the egg and sugar together in a separate bowl for at least 1 minute.
3. Stir the apple sauce into the egg and sugar mix. Then stir this mixture into the bowl of dry ingredients to make batter.
4. Stir in the cereal.

5. Spray the baking sheet evenly with the cooking spray. Pour in the batter. Bake for 15 minutes at 180° Celsius, Gas Mark 4. (A skewer pushed into the mixture should come out clean when the bars are done.)

6. Cut into bars with a sharp knife. Ease them out with a spatula and place on a cooling rack.

Link Also see the smoothie and fruit kebab recipes on pages 183–184.

Websites

Visit:

www.kidsdomain.com/craft/_sport.html for sports related craft activities

www.bbc.co.uk/cbbc/art/howto/fashion/ for fashion design tips and templates

www.bbc.co.uk/cbbc/sport/ for information on over 100 sports, and tips and advice on training

www.london2012.com/en for information on the 2012 Olympic Games

www.olympics.org.uk/home2.aspx the site of the British Olympic Association, with information about the Youth Games

www.olympic.org/uk/sports/index_uk.asp for the Olympic Movement list of official events

12 *Puzzles and problem solving*

Aspects of play

This theme has many strands. It covers puzzles and problem solving alongside lateral thinking and strategy.

Many of the activities are suitable for a wide age range as they can operate on many different levels. Take crosswords, for instance – they are equally enjoyed by children and adults. This theme can be greatly enhanced with the addition of the resources to support free play mentioned below.

Resources to support free play

- Jigsaw puzzles
- Board/strategy games
- Crosswords
- Word searches
- Sudoku
- Mazes
- Brainteasers
- Riddles (for details of how to source these see the website section on page 160)
- Paper and pens for games of hangman, noughts and crosses, battleships, and so on
- Labyrinths
- Magic sets
- Playing cards, etc.

Even within groups of a similar age, there's likely to be a wide range of literacy and numeracy ability, which is drawn upon in many puzzles including brainteasers and riddles. Ensure you provide activities to suit everyone. Remember it's as important to challenge children who excel at these activities as it is to provide for children who require simpler puzzles and/or more support.

Wink murder

ACTIVITY

*"*Play detective and solve the crime.*"*

Instructions

1. One child volunteers to be the detective, and leaves the room.

2. Everyone else stands in a circle, bowing their heads and closing their eyes.

3. Walk around the outside of the circle. En route, select one child to be the 'murderer' by tapping them on the shoulder. Continue to walk all the way around the circle so children have no clue who has been selected. The children can now open their eyes.

4. Call the detective back into the room. He or she must stand in the centre of the circle.

5. The object of the game is for the 'murderer' to 'kill' people by winking at them, without being caught by the detective. Players 'murdered' must scream and stage a dramatic death in which they eventually end up lying on the floor!

6. The detective must watch the players carefully to try to work out who the 'murderer' is. He or she is allowed three guesses which must be made by the time there are only three surviving players left.

7. If the detective guesses correctly, the murderer becomes the detective in the next round of the game. If the detective doesn't solve the crime he or she selects a new detective by tapping them on the shoulder as before.

Get knotted!

ACTIVITY

" *This game will have you tied up in knots!* **"**

Instructions

You need an even number of players, and no more than 12 participating in each 'knot'. You may have more than one knot in play at the same time.

1. The children stand in a circle facing inwards.
2. On your signal, everyone should close their eyes and reach their right hand across the circle. When they feel the hand of another player they should grasp it in the 'shaking hands' position. Players can now open their eyes.
3. Still holding right hands, players should reach out their left hands and grasp the free hand of a different player. (Everyone should now be holding hands with two different people.)
4. Without letting go hands, the group must now untangle themselves. This should eventually end in either one large circle or entwined circles with no 'knots'.

Getting knotted!

Puzzle partners

Equipment
- Assorted pictures
- Card
- Glue stick
- Scissors

Instructions

This activity is designed to get the children into teams. Once complete,
introduce a team game such as Playground word-search.

Link See pages 94–108 for further team activities.

1. This activity can be used to create any number of teams consisting of as
   many team members as you wish. We will take creating five teams of
   four members as our example.

2. Choose four pictures, one per team. You can get these from magazines,
   colouring books, the internet, etc. Back each picture with a sheet of card.

3. Cut each picture into four pieces, puzzle style.

4. If you want to create teams randomly, shuffle the pieces and distribute
   one per child. You may want to control who is in each team, to encourage
   the children to interact with new people for instance, or to ensure
   groupings are appropriate in terms of age. If so, write the children's
   initials on the back of each piece. Then shuffle the cards and distribute.

5. On your signal, the children should try to find the other three people who
   belong in their team. The first team to find one another and complete
   their jigsaw are the winners.

Playground word search

ACTIVITY

SPICE

"Can you devise and solve a giant sized word search?"

Equipment
- Chalk
- Metre ruler
- Example word search
- Pencil, paper and ruler

Instructions

1. Gather everyone around a table. Show them a word search, and check that everyone is familiar with how they work – children must find words hidden in the puzzle and draw a ring around them. Using the pencil, paper and ruler, demonstrate how a word search is made. (Draw a standard grid. Decide on a theme such as 'the beach' and write in relevant words, e.g. sand, sea, etc., diagonally, vertically and horizontally across the grid. Make a separate list of the words to be found alongside the grid as you go. Then fill the remaining spaces in the grid with random letters to disguise the themed words.)

2. Divide the group into two or more teams, and equip them with chalk and a metre ruler. Ask each team to choose a theme for their word search.

3. Head outside. Each team should find a space in the playground, and make their word search using the large ruler and chalk. Remind them to write a separate list of the words hidden next to the grid.

4. Teams should now swap positions and attempt to complete one another's word searches, drawing rings around the words they find with chalk.

Extension Idea

When working with older children, try giving teams the same playground puzzles to solve. Teams must try to beat their opponents. You may give (in chalk on the floor) a whole range of brainteasers to solve – see the website section on page 160 for details of sites with hundreds of them to choose from. Treasure hunts are another great activity for promoting teamwork and problem solving, and children love them. Some clues can be more cryptic than others to meet the needs of the whole team.

Invisible ink

"*Make invisible ink and write your own top-secret messages.*"

Equipment

- 1 lemon/lime
- Knife
- Juice squeezer
- White sheet of paper
- Cotton bud/cocktail stick
- Iron
- Tea towel

Instructions

To write an invisible message

1. Cut the lemon or lime in half. Squeeze out the juice.
2. Dip a cotton bud or cocktail stick into the mixture and 'write' on the paper. Re-dip as necessary to keep the tip wet. Leave the message to dry.

To read a secret message

1. Cover the paper with a tea towel to protect it.
2. Iron over the tea towel with a warm iron. Then remove the tea towel.
3. The message will be visible within a few minutes. (The carbon contained in lemon/lime juice darkens when it is heated.)

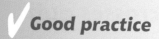

✔ Good practice

Closely supervise children when using an iron. Younger children will need their messages ironed for them.

Extension Idea

Older children can add more mystery to their messages by writing in code. To devise a simple but individual code, demonstrate the following method using paper and pen.

▶

1. Turn a sheet of paper to the landscape position. Write the letters of the alphabet along one edge.

2. Using the numbers 1–26, randomly enter a number under each letter as shown below.

A	B	C	D	E	F	G	H	I	J	K	L	M
12	10	21	19	4	25	9	14	3	11	5	18	1

N	O	P	Q	R	S	T	U	V	W	X	Y	Z
13	20	6	22	15	26	2	24	16	7	23	17	8

3. Explain that the numbers can be used to write a message, e.g. using the code above 'have fun' would be written '14 12 16 4 25 24 13'. It's important to leave a gap between each number, and a bigger gap between words, as shown here.

4. The children devise their own unique codes in the same way. They must give their 'secret contacts' a copy of their code key, so they will be able to decipher the messages they receive.

5. The children can now write coded messages, safe in the knowledge that, if they're intercepted, the secret message won't be revealed!

Noughts and crosses quiz

ACTIVITY

SPICE

"*Play team noughts and crosses with a difference.*"

Equipment
- Nine chairs
- Paper and pens
- Coin

Instructions

1. Prepare quiz questions to suit the group.

2. Split the group into two teams, the 'noughts' and the 'crosses'. Have one team draw nine noughts on paper (one per sheet), while the other team draws nine crosses.

3. Make a noughts and crosses style grid by placing nine chairs in three rows of three.
4. Each team will be asked a question in turn. Toss a coin to decide which team will answer the first question.
5. Teams may confer before answering a question. When a team answers correctly, one player should go and sit on a chair in the grid. They must hold up their nought or cross.
6. When a team has managed a row of three players on the grid, they have won the round. Keep track of the score on paper. Play an odd number of rounds if necessary to establish the winning team.

Snaky, snaky

"We search for a Snaky, Snaky champion!"

Instructions

1. This game is played in pairs. One child is the 'snaky'. Using one finger the snaky traces a wiggly line which represents a snake on the back of their partner, whilst saying this rhyme:

    Snaky, snaky on your back,

    Which finger did that?

2. The child's partner must guess which finger was used. If they guess correctly the children swap roles. If not, the snaky has another turn.

This game can be extended to include the whole group. It makes a great 5-minute time filler that needs no preparation.

Instructions

1. Have the group form a circle. Now ask players to turn sideways, so everyone is facing someone's back.
2. Choose a child to be the first snaky. He or she traces onto the back of the player in front of them.
3. If the player incorrectly guesses which finger was used, they are out and must leave the circle. The snaky stays in, and traces again on the back of the new person in front of them.

▶

4. However, if the player correctly guesses which finger was used, the snaky is out and leaves the circle. The player who guessed correctly is the new snaky, and traces onto the back of the person in front of them.

5. As children leave the game, the remaining players need to shuffle in to maintain the circle.

6. Continue until one player is left as the winner.

Guess who?

"Can you disguise celebrities in our fun challenge?"

ACTIVITY

SPICE

Equipment
- Pictures from newspapers/magazines
- Paper
- Scissors
- Felt-tip pens
- General craft resources (see below)
- Glue stick

Instructions

1. Divide the group into teams of three or four. Equip each team with newspapers/magazines and scissors.

2. Have each team select pictures of famous faces the group will recognise from newspapers and magazines. Cut them out, and mount each picture on paper. Each team should work in their own area, keeping their celebrity selection secret.

3. Using felt-tips and the craft resources, each team should 'disguise' their celebrities by adding any/all of the following:
   - a beard/moustache
   - sideburns
   - glasses
   - hat
   - new hair style
   - dentistry (blacking out teeth, adding a jewel, etc!).

   For example, pipe cleaners can be bent into the shape of glasses and stuck on.

4. Display the pictures on the wall gallery style, giving each a number.

5. Each team views the gallery in turn. They must guess which celebrities are depicted.

6. The team with the most correct answers are the winners.

7. Teams can also nominate one of their pictures for the title of 'The Funniest Disguise' – the group can then vote on the winner.

Extension Idea

Adapting the activity for older children:

1. When teams select their pictures from newspapers and magazines, have them choose photos of a comparable size. (Alternatively adjust the scale using a photocopier or scanner.)

2. Teams divide each face into three sections by drawing horizontal lines with a pencil and ruler. The first third should include the top of the head to the eyes, the second should feature the nose and cheeks, and the third should include the mouth and chin.

3. Teams swap the sections of faces around, assembling a new 'photo-fit' of 'merged' faces. For instance, a merged face may consist of Madonna's eyes, Nicole Kidman's nose and Matt Lucas' mouth.

4. The merged pictures are stuck to backing paper and displayed gallery style.

5. Opposing teams must view the gallery and guess the identity of the three merged celebrities.

6. Alternatively, swap the pictures of celebrities for printed out photographs of the children. It is easier to recognise the merged faces, but the 'photo-fits' will be the source of a lot of laughter!

Cheat!

"Cheating is allowed in this card game – just don't get caught!"

ACTIVITY

SPICE

Equipment
- Playing cards

▶

Instructions

1. This game works best with 4–8 players. The aim is to be the first player to get rid of all your cards. Suits don't matter; it's all about the numbers on the cards.

2. Shuffle the pack and deal out the whole deck. Players look at their own cards but keep them private.

3. Dealer plays first. You must select two or more cards of the same value (e.g. two cards, both eights) to put face-down on the centre of the table. In the unlikely event that you have no matching cards, a single card can be laid. The player laying the cards must describe them aloud, e.g. 'Two eights'.

4. The next player must put down one or more cards of the same value (eights) or a card one higher or one lower than the card on the table (in this case a seven or a nine). If they don't have the right cards, they must cheat by pretending that they do, e.g. a player may actually put down a three of clubs and a four of spades but declare, 'Two sevens'.

5. If another player suspects cheating, they can challenge by saying 'Cheat!' The cards last laid are then turned over. If the player is cheating, they must pick up the cards on the table. If not, the player who wrongly accused them of cheating must take the cards. Whoever picks up the cards starts the new round (as the dealer did previously). If the player is not accused of cheating, it's the next player's turn to lay cards. (In our example, sevens were laid last, so the new player must lay one or more sixes, sevens or eights, or pretend to).

6. Sometimes you are certain someone is cheating, e.g. you may have three sevens yourself so you know the other player can't have two sevens. But sometimes you'll think players just look guilty! You don't have to have evidence, just call 'Cheat!'

7. Players can also cheat by putting down more cards than they claim. So you may say, 'Two sevens', but sneak down three cards in the hope that nobody notices.

8. Picture cards are treated as others, e.g. if someone lays a jack you may lay a ten, jack or queen. If someone lays an ace you may lay a king, ace or two.

Cheating is the name of the game!

ACTIVITY

SPICE

Sitting, standing, bending, crouching

"Strike a pose to stay in the game . . ."

Equipment
- Chairs

Instructions

This game is for four players, but it's very funny to watch. You can call players up in turn to 'perform' the game in front of the group.

1. There is one rule – at any one time one player must be sitting, one standing, one bending down and one crouching. Start off by telling each player which of the poses they should adopt, and have them get into position.

▶

2. Give the players a subject to talk about, e.g. their favourite film. During the conversation players can casually adopt any of the other poses on a pretence, e.g. the player standing may bend to 'tie his shoe laces' or to 'talk to the person sitting'. Or the player crouching may 'get up to stretch'.

3. The other players must quickly adopt a new position while the talking continues, e.g. if the person standing bends down, the player previously bending must quickly stand up.

4. Any players may change position at any time.

Websites

Visit:

www.blackdog4kids.com/games/word/riddles.html for riddles for all ages

www.puzzles4kids.com/ to download printable word puzzles for children aged 8–11 years

www.activityvillage.co.uk/puzzles.htm to download word and logic puzzles, cryptograms, sudoku and mazes

www.vtaide.com/png/puzzles.htm for thinking games, slider puzzles and riddles for all ages

www.agameaday.com/0610/0610gemini1.htm for online brainteasers and anagrams for older children

13 The circus

Aspects of play

The smell of the greasepaint and the thrill of the crowd ... children love the circus! This theme is based on the modern animal-free circus, putting the spotlight on the skills of the performers.

Learning circus skills requires concentration, hand–eye co-ordination and perseverance. Mastering them is both challenging and fun, and boosts children's confidence and self-esteem. Participating can be soothing too – some people even meditate through juggling.

Resources to support free play

You can make circus equipment such as devil sticks and juggling balls (see the activities below), but it is advantageous to supplement this theme with some specialist equipment. However, this needn't be too costly. You can buy packs of spinning plates, juggling scarves and Diablo for about £5 each. They come with instructions. Peddle-goes (see the picture on page 170) and low stilts are around £25 each, but they're favourites during free play, whatever the theme. You may be able to borrow circus equipment from your local toy library.

✔ Good practice

Always ensure children have sufficient clear space for the activity they're working on. It's a good idea to appoint spotters – children can be so engrossed in activities such as balancing that they don't notice they're wondering out of the designated area. Ensure the necessary safety gear is worn when children ride bikes, skateboards, and so on.

Lasso

ACTIVITY

SPICE

"*Learn how to make and use a lasso.*"

Equipment

- A skipping rope with handles
- Scissors
- Felt-tip pen

Instructions

To make a lasso

1. You need a skipping rope with either plastic or wooden swivel handles (the rope spins inside the handle). You'll only need one handle on the lasso, so cut one handle off the skipping rope and discard.

2. Hold the lasso by the handle. Reach one-third of the way down the rope from the handle. Mark the one-third point with a felt-tip line.

3. Pick up the end of the rope without a handle. Tie it securely to the point you've marked, pulling the knot as tight as you can.

4. You can make several lassos of different lengths to meet the needs of the children in your group. Younger/shorter children will require shorter lassos so they don't skim the ground.

How to learn/teach lassoing

1. Always start with the rope hanging straight down.

2. Hold the handle in your preferred hand, using just the thumb and first two fingers.

3. Make small loops with the wrist (not the arm) until the rope starts to spin in a loop.

4. Be patient – spin too fast and it won't work. It takes a little practice.

Once you can spin the lasso, try to master slowly moving the arm up and down while still making small loops with the wrist. (Don't make loops with the arm, just up and down manoeuvres.)

162 *A Practical Guide to Activities for Older Children*

Making juggling balls

"Make your own juggling balls to take home."

Equipment
- Rice
- Balloons
- Scissors

Instructions

1. Cut the necks off two balloons.
2. Fill one with rice, packing it in until the balloon feels hard and the rubber is beginning to stretch.
3. Stretch the other balloon over the hole in the first balloon to seal it.
4. To make stronger balls, you can stretch over additional balloons in the same way (optional).

Extension Idea

Tennis balls are the ideal size for older children to juggle, but they are too light to have a dead drop, making them tricky to catch. You can adapt them as follows.

Equipment
- Tennis balls
- Rice
- Rubber glue
- Craft knife
- Kitchen scales

Instructions

1. Cut a 2 cm long slit into each ball with a craft knife.
2. Squeeze either side of the split to open a small hole.
3. Ask someone to pour in some rice for you while you hold the hole open. The ball should be filled halfway.
4. Squeeze the ball open again and apply strong glue suitable for rubber to either side of the split.
5. Stop squeezing and leave the glue to dry.

▶

6. As they get more adept at juggling, the children may prefer their balls a bit heavier. They can fill one tennis ball then throw and catch it for a while, adding more rice until they're comfortable with the weight. Then weigh the ball, so the other two (or more) balls can be made exactly the same weight.

✔ **Good practice**

Closely supervise the use of blades and strong glue, and only use them with older children.

ACTIVITY

Juggling workshop

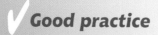

"*Learn how to juggle – it's lots of fun!*"

Instructions

How to learn/teach juggling

1. Start off by passing a ball from the right hand to the left and back again a few times. Then toss the ball back and forth. Stand centred with your feet firmly planted, holding your hands at waist level (as if you're carrying a tray).

2. When warmed up, throw the ball up with the right hand, aiming towards the left hand. The ball should peak above your left shoulder at about eye level before starting to drop. Then repeat in reverse, throwing from your left hand to your right hand, with the ball peaking above your right shoulder. It takes some practice to get the peak point right – sometimes the ball will go too high, sometimes too low to start with.

3. Repeat until you're comfortably passing one ball from right to left then left to right in a cycle.

4. Now pick up a second ball and hold one in each hand. Remember to stand correctly. Throw the first ball from your right hand towards your left hand as before. Just as the ball reaches its peak, throw the second ball under the first, towards your right hand. Catch the ball falling towards your left hand, then the one falling towards your right hand.

5. Now repeat in reverse – throw the ball in your left hand towards your right hand. As it peaks, throw the second ball under the first towards your left hand. Catch the ball falling towards your right hand, then the one falling towards your left hand.

6. Keep practising steps 4 and 5 until you can do them comfortably in a cycle. Some people learn within 10 minutes, others have to practise regularly to get the hang of it. Learning to juggle smoothly with two balls is the hardest part. Once the technique is mastered, it's easier to learn how to juggle with additional balls.

7. Now try three balls. Hold two in your right hand and one in your left. Throw one ball from your right hand to your left. When it peaks, throw the second ball in your left hand under the first towards your right hand. When that ball peaks, throw the remaining ball in your right hand. Keep practising!

Top tips

- Teach younger/struggling children to juggle with net scarves. The principle is the same as when juggling with balls, but the motion is slowed down.
- If children can't help but walk forwards when juggling, they can practise in front of a wall.
- Everyone drops balls a lot when learning! At home children can practise over their bed so it's easier to pick them up.

Group juggling game

"Join in to juggle dozens of balloons!"

Equipment
- Balloons

Instructions

1. Inflate some balloons. You need at least as many balloons as there are children, plus half again, i.e. for 20 children you would need 20 + 10 = 30 balloons (round up odd numbers). Have a few spare balloons handy. ▶

2. Explain that the group must work together to keep all the balloons in the air by 'juggling' (patting) them. The balloons mustn't touch the floor, and mustn't be held.

3. Introduce the balloons to the group two or three at a time. Keep a note of how many balloons are successfully juggled at each turn – the group can then try to beat their own best score.

4. This game even works well with very large numbers of participants. Adults and children can play together too, so it's well suited to special events such as family play days where it can be enjoyed by dozens of players at once.

Making devil sticks

"Help to make devil sticks for our circus supplies box.**"**

ACTIVITY

SPICE

Equipment
- 60 cm length of 14 mm dowel
- 45 cm length of 11.5 mm dowel
- Insulation tape in two colours
- Walking stick end/rubber tape
- Fabric remnants
- Glue

Instructions

1. Find the centre of the dowel and mark it by wrapping some insulation tape around the dowel at this point. (You'll need to see the middle easily when using the stick later.)

2. Using a different colour to the one used in step 1, wrap the whole stick in insulation tape from each end into the middle. You may like to use extra colours for decoration.

3. The ends of the stick must be covered in rubber. Use rubber tape, or fit a small rubber walking stick end – you may need to cover the end of the stick in layers of insulation tape before the walking stick end will fit snugly.

4. Check the weight distribution of the stick is even by balancing it across two fingers. If not, add more tape to the light end until balanced.

5. Lay a strip of fabric horizontally on the table. Make into a fringe by cutting slits at regular intervals along the fabric. The slits should be one-third of the fabric deep. Using pinking shears will prevent fraying.

6. Repeat on the second fabric strip.

7. Apply glue to one end of the stick. Attach one fabric fringe by sticking down along the straight edge (the edge without the slits). Repeat on the other end and leave to dry. (See diagram below.)

8. The remaining dowels will be the hand-sticks. Cover these decoratively in insulation tape.

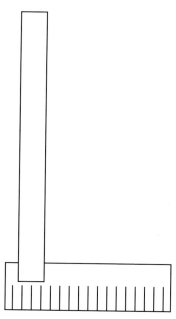

Stick the straight edge of the fringe to the devil stick.

Devil stick

Devil stick workshop

"Learn how to do devil stick tricks!"

ACTIVITY

Instructions

How to learn/teach tricks

1. The devil stick is controlled by the two hand-sticks. Kneel down on one knee. Take one hand-stick in each hand as though you're going to play the drums.

2. Put the devil stick on the floor on its end, and rest it against one of the hand-sticks. It should touch the hand-stick at the midway point between the centre of the devil-stick (marked with tape) and the top of the devil stick. This means the devil stick will be at an angle.

3. Lift the hand-stick acting as a rest upwards – the devil stick will fall onto the opposite hand-stick. Now move this hand-stick upwards to send the devil stick back. The devil stick must always be struck above the mid-way point. The movement must be vertical, lifting motions, similar to the motion made when lifting a drumstick from a drum.

4. Repeat, building momentum and it's possible to lift the devil stick from the floor and continue moving it back and forth. This is the most basic trick, known as the 'Tick-Tock'. Once achieved, children can try more complicated moves. See the website section on page 172 for details of sites where you can download trick instructions and see some tricks performed on video.

Balancing act

"Balancing objects"

Equipment
- Peacock feather
- Pole
- Ball, etc. (see below)

Instructions

To learn/teach balancing an object

1. A peacock feather is the easiest thing to balance, so start with this if possible. Hold your preferred hand out and place the feather upright on your palm or fingertip, holding it steady with your other hand.

2. Looking at the top of an object and never the bottom is the key to successful balancing. Look at the top, then let go with your supporting hand. Move your hand so it stays directly under the top of the object – you must keep the bottom of the object centred under the top to balance successfully. (Keep looking at the top.)

3. You will need to move around the room to keep balancing the object.

4. Try some different objects such as balls, poles, dowels, and so on. With practice you can balance so many objects. Top-heavy objects such as a tennis racket should be balanced with the heavy end on top. Small, light objects, such as straws or pencils are most difficult to balance – but these don't look so impressive anyway!

5. You can also try balancing objects on your chin, forehead and feet. The principle is always the same – look at the top of the object and keep the bottom centred under it.

To learn/teach balancing yourself

1. Get into the hands and knees position, as if about to crawl.
2. Look in front and fix your eyes on a point on the wall. Keep looking at it – this helps balance.
3. To balance on three points, bring one arm out straight in front of you. (If right handed raise the left arm, if left handed raise the right arm).
4. To balance on two points, keep the arm raised and eyes fixed, and extend your opposite leg behind you.
5. See if you can extend the other arm without starting to keel over!

To learn/teach balancing on the tightrope

To simulate walking the high wire, you can lay a length of cord across the room for children to test their balancing skills – the thicker and rounder the cord, the better. Holding arms out helps balance.

To learn/teach balancing acts

Once children can balance in several ways, they can devise a balancing routine to perform. The spinning of plates is achieved with a combination of balancing and motion, making this a good trick to incorporate.

Spinning plates requires balance and motion

Circus performance

A performance can be organised once the children have mastered a few circus skills. Appoint one or more ringmaster – it's a good job for children reluctant to perform. Ringmasters can decide the running order of acts, and plan how to build excitement when introducing them. Terms like 'death defying', 'beyond belief' and 'amazing antics' should come in handy!

You can even have performances inside your own big top – see the page opposite for details. Circus posters can be made and displayed, and tickets can be issued if desired (this appeals to younger children).

Extension Idea

Older children can incorporate their existing skills into a circus performance. These might include double-dutch skipping, doing stunts on a skateboard or bike, or performing yo-yo tricks. In addition, they can learn skills such as riding a peddle-go or spinning plates, depending on your resources.

Clowning around is also great fun! Older children can design routines and sketches with plenty of pratfalls and slapstick fun – props such as buckets full of shredded gossamer can be used to simulate throwing water over the crowd. Also see page 31 for face painting details.

Link

Mastering the 'peddle-go' bike

Big top

""Make a big top and perform inside.""

Equipment
- Large parachute

ACTIVITY

S P I C E

Instructions

To create the big top

1. Spread out the parachute on the floor. Have children form a circle around it and pick it up. Adults can join in too.

2. The group should raise and lower arms in unison to mushroom the parachute. Do this several times to build momentum.

3. Meanwhile, explain that to make the big top the group must work together. You will shout out 'Now!' when the parachute is mushroomed in the air. Instead of just lowering their arms to bring the parachute down, this time each player will pull their section of parachute over their head down to their bottom, and quickly sit on the floor, trapping the edge of the parachute beneath them.

4. Have a practice. You may need three or four goes before everyone gets the hang of it.

5. When you've successfully made the big top, have an adult stand in the middle to act as a 'tent pole' if necessary, holding up the middle of the tent should it sag.

Using the big top

1. The children can now perform inside the big top. However it does get hot and stuffy inside quite quickly, so you may want to keep performances short but frequent, returning to the tent for instalments of the show throughout the session, day or week.

2. The big top is also an atmospheric place to hear stories about the circus, whether made up by the group or told/read to them. See pages 32–33 for a method of devising a story with groups of children.

Circus food

Link

Popcorn, toffee apples and sweets are all popular circus fare. See pages 62–63 for recipes.

✔ Good practice

Ask the children to let you know if they feel too hot and bothered and wish to leave the big top at any time. Children with respiratory difficulties such as asthma may be less tolerant of the atmosphere inside.

Any equipment needed for a performance (such as juggling balls) can be prepared before the big top is created. Simply place equipment under the centre of the parachute before it is picked up by the group. Ensure equipment is returned there before the big top is deflated so it doesn't become a trip hazard. Acts needing a lot of room (such as balancing acts) are not suited to the big top.

Extension Idea

You may like to consider inviting a professional to run a circus skills workshop. Professionals will have the expertise to coach children in more complex skills, which will be particularly relevant to older children. And when the circus is in town, make contact. Many owners are happy to give a tour of the big top between performances.

Websites

Visit:

www.stixguru.com/new/home.htm and **www.devilstick.de/ english/home.htm** to learn tricks and watch online videos of devil stick performers in action

www.yo-yoguy.com to learn yo-yo tricks, for beginners to advanced

www.webtech.kennesaw.edu/jcheek3/circus.htm for circus information and colouring pages

www.web.superb.net/cardtric/tricks.htm to learn card tricks for beginners to advanced

14 *The rainforest*

Aspects of play

Tall trees and wild vegetation grow freely alongside exotic plants and tropical fruits. It's home to snakes, monkeys, orang-utans, big cats and exotic birds to name just a few. It's no wonder children enjoy a theme that celebrates our fascinating rainforests.

Since many people never set foot in a real rainforest, why not embark on an art project to recreate one in your setting? The project can encourage research and creativity, promote imaginative play and provide the perfect backdrop to the theme.

You can provide artistic inspiration by offering access to related pictures featured in books and websites. This will help children to develop their own creative ideas about how to make the rainforest installation. Some additional art and craft suggestions are provided below.

Resources to support free play

- Art and craft supplies
- Play animal figures
- Real plants
- Related fiction and non-fiction books
- Internet access
- Sound effects CD (available from libraries)

Rainforest art

" Help to recreate a rainforest
in our ambitious art project. *"*

SPICE

Rainforests have four layers known as 'strata'. Thinking in terms of these gives focus to a rainforest art project.

Strata 1: the forest floor

Equipment
- Fabric
- Fabric dye
- Playground bark (optional)
- Pipe cleaners
- Self-adhesive wobbly eyes

Instructions
1. Old sheets dyed brown can be used to represent the forest floor. Follow the instructions on a packet of cold or machine dye. Then spread the dry fabric on the floor, in front of some wall space that can also be dedicated to the display.
2. A little playground bark scattered on top adds both texture and a woody fragrance (available from educational suppliers/large DIY stores).
3. The forest floor is home to numerous insects. The children can fashion their own mini-beasts from pipe-cleaners, finished off with wobbly-eyes. Display these on the forest floor.

Strata 2: the understory
To create a giant collage in the space between the forest floor and the top of the tree trunks:

Equipment
- Green backing paper
- Rainforest pictures
- Paper
- Pencils
- Scissors
- Felt-tip pens, paints, etc.
- Sticky-tack

Instructions

1. Fix the backing paper to the wall.

2. Referring to pictures in books and so on, the children draw rainforest creatures, plants and vegetation, cut them out and fix them overlapping slightly to the background. The collage can be added to throughout the theme.

3. The tree trunks will also occupy the foreground of the understory – see below.

Rainforest art installation

Strata 3: the canopy

To create the treetop area where monkeys play:

Equipment
- Thin card in green and brown
- Earth
- Play bucket
- Sticky tape
- Scissors
- Pencil

▶

Instructions

1. To make the trunk, take a sheet of brown card at least 80 cm long. Roll it into a tube.
2. One child should hold the tube to prevent it unrolling while another cuts several 2 cm deep slits all the way around one end to make a fringe.
3. With one child still holding the tube steady, the other takes a firm grip and pulls the inside of the tube from the top until the trunk extends to its full height.
4. Stick down the edges with sticky tape.
5. Draw palm tree leaves of approximately 40 × 20 cm on the green card and cut them out. Allow 3–5 leaves per tree. If you decide to make taller trees, adjust the size of the leaves accordingly.
6. Secure the leaves to the trunk with sticky tape.
7. To display the tree, push the trunk into a bucket of earth. This also adds to the fragrance of the rainforest area.

Canopy vines

Equipment
- Cord
- Paint
- Paintbrushes
- Masking tape

Instructions

1. Paint cord green and brown to resemble vines. Leave to dry.
2. Hang from one tree to another, securing with tape.

Spiral snakes

These look great both hanging from trees and on the forest floor.

Equipment
- Dinner plate
- Paper/fun-foam
- Pencil
- Scissors
- Sticky tape
- Paint/felt-tip pens/decorative craft resources

Instructions

1. Place a dinner plate on a piece of paper or fun-foam and draw around it. Using this as a guide for the outer circle, place the pencil on the paper/foam and spiral inwards until the middle of the paper is reached.
2. Cut along the line, creating a coil.
3. Decorate as desired. Paper snakes can be painted or coloured. Additional craft resources such as sequins, fun-foam scraps and self-adhesive wobbly eyes can also be used.
4. Draw and cut out a paper forked-tongue. Stick to the head with sticky-tape.
5. Cut the tail end into a V-shape.
6. Hang from the ceiling or a tree.

Strata 4: the emergents

To create giant trees higher than canopy height, home to more birds and insects:

Equipment
- Large cardboard tubes (see below)
- Stiff card
- Pencil
- Paint
- Paintbrushes
- Heavy-duty stapler
- Earth compost
- Bucket

Instructions

1. For the tree trunk you need a large cardboard tube, such as the insert from a large roll of paper or carpet. Paint the tube brown.
2. Draw the shape of a treetop onto stiff card and cut it out.
3. Paint the treetop green.
4. When the paint is dry, staple the treetop to the trunk. Younger children will need help with this task.
5. Push the trunk into a bucket of compost to display.

Polly parrots

Equipment
- Card
- Paper
- Felt-tip pens
- String
- Sticky-tape
- Drawing pins

Instructions

1. Draw and cut out the body of a parrot in profile. Decorate with felt-tips.
2. Decorate a sheet of paper, then fold it into a fan.
3. Cut a slit into the body where the wings would be. Pass the folded fan halfway through.
4. Open out the fan wings and suspend from the ceiling with string. You may also like to draw and decorate some butterflies to hang up.

As a finishing touch, why not add any appropriate soft toys or model animals you have to the area? Children may also like to paint some larger animals such as monkeys or panthers on stiff card, and find places to hang or stand them. Play a recording of rainforest sounds to add to the atmosphere.

Extension Idea

Groups of older children may enjoy inviting a group of small children (such as a pre-school group) to experience their rainforest and hear a related story in situ.

Soft toys can enhance the effect

Tiger tails game

❝Can you keep your tail and win the game?❞

Equipment
- Strips of fabric/ribbon

Instructions

1. Each player needs to wear a 'tail'. Tails should be represented by a strip of fabric or piece of ribbon tucked into the waistband of each player's clothes.

2. Starting on your signal, the object of the game is for each player to run around trying to collect as many tails as possible by pulling them from other players' waistbands. Simultaneously players must try not to lose their own tail.

▶

3. The game is over when only one player is left with a tail. Each player should count up how many tails they have, scoring one point per tail. The player left with their own tail scores three bonus points. The player with the most points wins.

ACTIVITY

Ling ching luk (Monkey run for a tree)

SPICE

"Get ready for some monkey business!"

Equipment
● Access to trees (real or props)

Instructions
This game from Thailand is traditionally played in woodland areas, so it lends itself well to this theme. If you don't have access to trees at your setting you can play using props – see the instructions on page 175.

1. Choose a volunteer to be the 'monkey'. The monkey should stand away from the immediate area of trees.

2. All other players must begin the game touching a tree. There must only be one player per tree throughout the game. In the event that you are surrounded by trees, only the ones selected by the children at the start of the game are in play.

3. Shout 'Ling ching luk!' or 'Monkey run for a tree!' to start the game. On this signal, players must begin running, changing places constantly, pausing for just a few seconds to tag trees, before moving on again. There must still be only one player per tree at any given moment.

4. Meanwhile, the monkey must attempt to touch a vacant tree. (He or she must be constantly on the move – 'guarding' trees or players is not allowed.) When the monkey succeeds, any players without a tree at that moment must scramble to a vacant one. The monkey and the player left without a tree should change places. The game starts again with the new monkey.

Snakes alive!

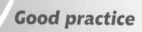

"You'll be slithering like a snake in this team game!**"**

Instructions

1. You need at least five players, but no more than eight should play in each 'snake'.

2. Players stand one behind the other in a 'snake'. The player at the front is the 'head' of the snake, the player at the back is the 'tail'. All but the head should hold the waist of the player in front with both hands.

3. The head should attempt to catch the tail – this involves lots of twisting and turning that the players in the middle must keep up with.

4. When the head catches the tail, players should move along one position in the snake. The head will go to the back and become the tail. Continue until all the children have been both the head and the tail.

Link   Also see the 'Snaky, snaky' game on page 155.

✔ Good practice

'Snakes alive' is great fun, but best suited to over-8s. Tell players to let go of the player in front if they feel too pulled at any point.

Animal tag

"This game calls for animal impressions – the louder the better!**"**

SPICE

Instructions

1. The children form a large circle. One player is selected to be 'it' – he or she stands in the centre of the circle.

2. 'It' shouts 'Go!' On this signal, all players start to make the animal noise of their choice, and should continue until the word 'change' is called (see step 5).

3. Any two children making the same noise must run across the circle to exchange places. If more than two children make the same noise, they must keep swapping places until all of them have changed position.

4. 'It' must try to tag one of the moving players before they rejoin the circle.

5. The tagged player becomes the new 'it'. He or she shouts 'Change!' On this signal, each player makes a new noise, and so the game continues. If 'it' doesn't manage to tag another player, he or she shouts 'change' themselves and has another attempt.

In mixed age groups, younger children may find it difficult to tag older children. You can overcome this by introducing the rule that if an adult makes a Tarzan cry, all players must swap places with the child on their right. This allows an adult to give 'it' an advantage.

Extension Idea

To make the game more difficult for an older 'it', you can have them stand within the circle alongside other players, rather than in the middle.

Tropical treats

"Make and enjoy some terrific tropical treats."

Fruit kebab buffet

Equipment
- Tropical fruit
- Skewers
- Knives
- Plates
- Serviettes
- Yoghurt (optional)

Instructions

1. Purchase a range of tropical fruits. Include favourites alongside exotic fruits the children may not have tried before – star fruit, for instance.
2. Prepare the fruit for eating (washing, peeling, stoning, etc.), then cut into chunks.
3. Set the fruit out on plates, buffet style.
4. Equip each child with a skewer so they can select chunks of fruit and push them on to make a kebab. The children will need serviettes as eating fruit kebabs can be a messy affair! You can also offer yoghurt for dipping.

> ✔ **Good practice**
>
> If using a skewer is inappropriate for anyone in your group, stick to soft fruit and use a drinking straw instead.

Slush cocktails

Equipment
- Tropical fruit juices
- Ice cube trays
- Access to freezer
- Citrus fruit/drink decoration
- Knife

▶

- Freezer bags and rolling pin OR ice-crusher/blender (see below)
- Tablespoon
- Glasses/beakers
- Straws

Instructions

1. If you have access to a juicer and can create your own juices with the children, do so. If not, purchase cartons of juice in at least three different flavours, and ideally different colours.
2. Pour juice into ice-cube trays and freeze until solid.
3. Prepare slices of citrus fruit to be used as glass decorations later.
4. If you have access to an ice-crusher or an electric blender, use the machine to crush each flavour of juice separately. If not, place the frozen ice-cubes in freezer bags and seal them, using a separate bag for each flavour. Crush the ice with a rolling pin.
5. Use a tablespoon to layer the different flavours of crushed ice in tall glasses or beakers.
6. The cocktails can be left as 'slush' or chilled juice can be added.
7. Add a straw and the citrus fruit to the glasses. You may like to add other cocktail decorations such as umbrellas.

Tropical breakfast smoothies

Equipment
For two child-sized drinks:
- 1 banana
- 1 peach/nectarine
- Half a cup of milk
- 1 tablespoon yoghurt
- Ice
- 1 tablespoon natural bran
- 1 teaspoon honey
- Glasses/beakers

Instructions

1. Peel the fruit. Stone the peach/nectarine.
2. Slice the fruit and place in the blender.
3. Add the rest of the ingredients. Blend until smooth.
4. Place ice in tall glasses. Pour on the blended mixture.

Tropical smoothies are great for breakfast clubs

Making masks

"Make magnificent masks to take home."

Equipment
- Newspaper
- PVA glue
- Water
- Bucket
- Card
- Recycled materials (boxes, etc.)
- Pencil
- Scissors
- Masking tape

Instructions

1. Make papier-mâché: mix together a generous solution of one part PVA glue and one part water in a bucket. Tear newspaper into shreds and submerge in the solution. Leave to soak for 30 minutes.

▶

2. Draw a mask shape onto card and cut it out, remembering holes for the eyes.

3. Use recycled materials to make 3D features. For instance, sections of egg cartons make good noses, etc. Awkward shapes such as ears can be cut from corrugated card. Stick the features in place with masking tape.

4. Cover the entire mask with papier-mâché strips. Smooth the strips over the features so just 3D contours are seen. Leave to dry overnight.

5. You may like to add a second layer of papier-mâché for durability and a better finish (optional). Leave to dry overnight.

6. Paint and decorate the mask as desired.

Extension Idea

Older children can make masks with a real sense of drama. The following method was originally used to make masks for stage actors. Older children may like to look at the impressive Lion King stage masks for inspiration. See the website section on page 188.

Equipment
- Plaster cast bandages
- Scissors
- Petroleum jelly
- Bowl
- Warm water
- Acrylic paints
- Paintbrushes
- Elastic

Instructions

1. The children should work in pairs, taking it in turns to make a mask and to be a model.

2. The model should close their eyes while their face is smeared evenly in a layer of petroleum jelly. The bridge of the nose and the eyebrows should be covered, while the eye area and lips must be avoided. Hair should be kept well out of the way throughout the activity.

3. Plaster bandages can be bought from educational suppliers and craft shops. Cut bandages into lengths of approximately 15 cm.

4. Hold a strip of bandage from the top with one hand. Dip into a bowl of warm water, then remove and hold above the bowl.

5. With the thumb and forefinger of the other hand, grasp the plaster and wipe downwards from top to bottom to squeeze out excess water.

6. Place the strip gently on the model's face, from the top of the forehead to the bottom of the chin. Smooth out gently and cut off the surplus carefully. (The petroleum jelly will prevent the cast from sticking to the face.)

7. Repeat the process, laying some strips horizontally and some vertically until the whole face is covered except the eye area, nostrils and lips, which must be avoided. Gently smooth the edges of the bandages with a damp hand to blend them together.

8. Leave the mask to set on the face for a few minutes.

9. When hard, loosen the mask by wiggling it gently, then ease from the face.

10. Models must remove all traces of plaster and petroleum jelly by washing their faces thoroughly.

11. The mask can be painted with acrylic paint.

12. Add elastic for wearing, or display masks on the wall.

✔ Good practice

Check that children are not allergic to petroleum jelly or plaster beforehand. Ensure the environment and children are well-covered for this messy activity.

Environmental issues

This theme provides a good opportunity for promoting awareness of environmental issues such as the conservation of animals and the protection of natural environments. You may like to invite an appropriate visitor to talk to the group, and perhaps research local schemes that the group could become involved in – a recycling scheme for instance, or planting trees.

Websites

Visit:

www.discovery.com search 'rainforest' for numerous links, including footage from a web-cam positioned in a rainforest

www.enchantedlearning.com/subjects/rainforest/animals/ Rfbiomeanimals.shtml for rainforest facts, animal profiles and printouts

www.disney.co.uk/MusicalTheatre/TheLionKing/abouttheshow/ behind-costumesmasks.html to view masks from the musical The Lion King

15 *Dinosaurs*

Aspects of play

Dinosaurs have captured the curiosity of children for generations. Where better than the play setting to fuel this natural interest?

A flexible approach to this theme will allow individual children to follow their own interests at a level that suits them, as they find out as little or as much as they'd like about prehistoric times. For instance, during a craft activity in which children create their own skeleton fossils (see page 193), some children may spend time on the design of the skeleton, sketching it out and perhaps finding pictures in books to copy. Other children may randomly assemble a few bones, preferring to spend the majority of their time squishing the delightfully messy mix of compost through their fingers.

Activities such as the dinosaur egg hunt are exciting, and such pastimes create even more interest in the subject matter. The imagination of children can take over as they engage in creative activities such as dressing-up – they needn't be concerned by historical facts as they imagine what it was like to be a huge dinosaur stomping across the land – unless of course, they want to be …

Resources to support free play

- Dinosaur toys
- Pictures/posters
- Textbooks suitable for the age range
- Internet access
- Sand/earth and digging materials (for mock fossil digs)
- Modelling materials such as clay
- Related fiction and non-fiction books

Dinosaur egg hunt

"Make and hatch your own dinosaur egg, complete with a baby dinosaur and fossil!"

Equipment

To make approximately six eggs:

- Small plastic dinosaur toys
- 2½ cups flour
- 1 cup coffee granules
- 1½ cups salt
- 1 cup play sand
- Measuring cups
- Bowl, wooden spoon
- Water
- Access to an oven (optional)

Instructions

1. You'll need one small, hard plastic dinosaur toy per child. These can be purchased cheaply by the packet, and are often sold as party-bag fillers.

2. Make a batch of dough, which will be used to make the eggs. This recipe is designed to give dough a rock-like appearance and texture when it dries. Mix the flour in a bowl with the coffee granules. Add the salt and play sand. From a cup of water, gradually stir in a little at a time until the mixture starts to hold together. Now knead the mixture by hand until it becomes solid, adding a little more water if necessary.

3. Mould dough *firmly* around a dinosaur, working it into an egg shape. The dinosaur should be completely covered in dough, but avoid making eggs too large or you will have difficulty drying them out.

4. Remember to identify which egg belongs to which child before removing them for hardening. Eggs can be air-dried on a windowsill, but it will take a couple of days. Alternatively, you can bake the eggs gently in the oven on a very low heat, turning as necessary until hard. This takes around 30 minutes. Don't be tempted to turn up the heat, or the dinosaurs may melt.

5. Once the hardened eggs have cooled, practitioners can hide them in the outside play space.

6. Send the children to find their own egg and one stone each. (They should ignore the other eggs they come across.) The children can gently chip away at their egg with the stone in order to hatch their dinosaur. Tell them to remove their dinosaur carefully, and they should see the imprint of the dinosaur left inside the shell. They often like to keep both the dinosaur and their eggshell 'fossil'.

7. You may like to use the dinosaurs and eggs in a 'prehistoric habitat' – see page 196.

✓ Good practice

It can be challenging to supervise children outside when they're searching all over the play space for eggs. Engaged in their hunt, young children may be more likely to inadvertently stray beyond the boundaries of the setting. Deploy practitioners at the exit points for security.

Extension Idea

Although children will grow out of making dinosaur eggs and playing with figures, you may be surprised to find that even the oldest children are happy to hunt for hidden chocolate and the like! Try hiding wrapped dinosaur-shaped sweets or wrapped chocolate eggs around the setting for this age group.

Prehistoric play

ACTIVITY

S P I C E

Giant Jurassic game

❝Test your dinosaur knowledge in our giant board game, where you become the counter!❞

Equipment

- Research materials (books, internet access)
- Index cards and pens
- Chalk

Instructions

1. Research facts and figures about dinosaurs and write them on the index cards, one per card. Write the word 'true' on each card.

2. Make up some false dinosaur facts. Some may be funny, others may seem plausible. Write the word 'false' on each card.

3. Using chalk, draw a giant game board directly on the floor. It should mimic the traditional figure of eight tabletop game board, as shown in the diagram below. Mark on the start and finish lines. The size of the board will determine how many children can play the game at once. It's suggested you make each square of the board large enough to accommodate at least four children.

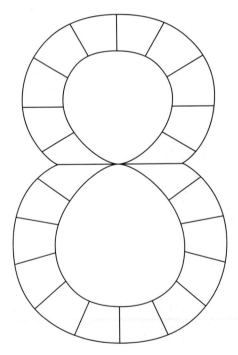

Figure of eight gameboard

4. The players should stand at the start line. One or more children should become quiz masters. It's their job to read one fact from the cards to the players. Each player must then guess if the fact is true or false.

5. The quiz masters should reveal whether the fact is true or false. All players who answered correctly may move forward three spaces. All players who answered incorrectly must remain where they are.

6. Rounds of the game should continue until all players cross the finish line.

7. You may like to try variations to allow the children to play in teams. For example, you could divide the children into four groups, each represented by one child 'counter'. The teams could confer before answering true or false. Alternatively, the children may play in pairs, standing on the game board together.

Extension Idea

Link

For older children, dinosaur questions can be used in conjunction with the 'Noughts and crosses quiz'.
See page 154 for instructions.

ACTIVITY

S P I C E

Skeleton fossils

"Create a 'fossilised skeleton' to take home."

Equipment
- Macaroni
- Freezer bags
- Rolling pin
- PVA glue and brushes
- Compost (child-friendly)
- Bowl, measuring cups, tablespoon
- Paper plates
- Paper and crayons

Instructions

1. Put a handful of macaroni into a freezer bag. Break into pieces by hammering the bag lightly with the end of a rolling pin. (The pasta should be broken, not crushed!)

2. Add 5 tablespoons of PVA glue to 1½ cups of compost, and mix together by hand. The mixture should be solid enough to hold together in a rough ball shape. Add more glue if necessary.

3. The mixture will be used to represent the earth. Place a ball of the mixture onto a paper plate. Press it out by hand until the plate is covered – the mixture should now be about 2 cm thick.

4. Push the macaroni pieces into the earth in the pattern of a dinosaur skeleton. The children may like to refer to pictures of real skeleton fossils for inspiration.

5. When finished, seal and varnish the model by brushing a coat of PVA glue over the entire surface. The glue will dry clear. There may be some smudging of compost over the macaroni, but this will add to the effect.

6. When the model is dry, peel away the paper plate. The children may like to mark their initials on the bottom of their models. The underneath can now be sealed as before. Leave to dry.

7. The children can take rubbings of their skeletons by covering them with paper and colouring over with crayons.

8. The models can also be hidden in the sand tray to be discovered on a 'fossil dig'.

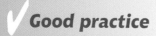 **Good practice**

Ensure the children wash their hands thoroughly afterwards. Clean the work surfaces with disinfectant.

 **Extension Idea**

Older children can construct 3D balsawood skeletons, which can be purchased as kits from craft shops.

Triceratops hoopla

"Can you hook a hoop on the horn of a triceratops?"

Equipment

- Sheet of block-board or ply, edges sanded
- 3 x 30 cm lengths of 12 mm wide dowel, ends sanded
- Hand drill with 12 mm drill bit
- Wood glue (child friendly)
- Pencils
- Poster paint
- Hoops
- Chalk

Instructions

1. Draw the face of a triceratops on a sheet of block-board or ply. The horns will be represented by lengths of dowel, so for now, leave a gap where the horns should be.

2. Using a hand drill, make three holes in the board for the dowel.

3. Following the directions on your brand of wood glue, stick the dowel into position and leave to dry.

4. Decorate the triceratops with paint and other craft materials if desired.

5. The aim of the game is to toss hoops onto the dowels. Players traditionally have three attempts per turn. If you don't have suitably light hoops amongst your resources, embroidery hoops make a good substitute. They are lightweight, affordable and available in a range of sizes.

6. Place the hoopla on the floor. Draw a chalk line a few paces away for players to stand behind when they throw their hoops.

 Good practice

Children need close one-to-one supervision when using the hand drill and wood glue. Ensure the wood glue is safe for children's use – an age limit will be specified. Always put woodwork equipment away securely immediately after use.

Extension Idea

Target games can be made harder for older children by asking players to throw from further away, using smaller hoops or awarding points for different dowels.

Prehistoric habitats

"Create a prehistoric habitat complete with an erupting volcano!"

Method 1: habitat in a box

Equipment
- Cardboard boxes
- Scissors
- Glue sticks
- Sticky-tape
- Plasticine
- Felt-tip pens
- Paint and brushes
- Camera film canisters
- Baking powder
- Vinegar
- Teaspoon
- Food colouring (optional)
- Assorted craft resources, such as paper, cellophane, pipe cleaners, tissue paper

Instructions

1. Turn an empty cardboard box on its side. Cut away the top panel, leaving a back, two sides and a bottom. This will provide the structure of the prehistoric scene. The children may like to work in pairs or small groups, depending on the size of the boxes available.

2. Paint the structure in base colours such as grey, green and brown. Leave to dry.

3. Decorate the structure as desired, using a range of craft resources imaginatively to create a dinosaur habitat. For example, bushes can be

created by sticking scrunched up green tissue paper to the bottom of the box. Tree trunks may be made by pushing a pipe cleaner into some Plasticine. Treetops can be drawn on paper with felt-tips, cut out and fixed onto the trunk with sticky-tape. Plasticine can be used to make caves, hills and mountains. Foil can represent water.

4. Populate with dinosaurs, and the habitat is ready for play. You can model dinosaurs from Plasticine, or use ready-made toys.

5. To create a volcano, stick an empty film canister down with Plasticine (which allows it to be removed and replaced as necessary). Use more Plasticine on the outside of the canister to sculpt the sloping shape of a volcano. Place a teaspoon of baking powder in the canister. Make the volcano bubble by adding a teaspoon of vinegar. You can make the volcano erupt and the lava flow by increasing the ingredients. You may like to add a drop of red or yellow food colouring for effect, but be aware that if in contact colouring will stain skin temporarily and the habitat permanently.

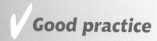

✓ Good practice

Link

See page 5 for instructions on sterilising film canisters before using them for play purposes.

Method 2: prehistoric play mat

Equipment
- Plain cotton fabric
- Pencils and erasers
- Fabric paints, crayons or felt-tip pens

Instructions

1. These washable play mats can be used again and again in free play, long after the dinosaur theme is over. For durability, the fabric used should be hemmed or cut with pinking shears to prevent fraying. Read the instructions on your brand of fabric paint in advance of the activity – you may need to wash material (even if it's new) prior to painting it.

2. Distribute the fabric. The children may like to work on their own, creating a play mat each to take home, in which case, lengths of fabric approximately 60 cm square are ideal. Alternatively, small groups may make larger mats to be kept at the setting. You could even have the whole group working collaboratively to turn a sheet into a giant play mat. ▶

3. With a pencil, design the play mat by drawing on land, sea, trees, bushes, caves, mountains, and so on.

4. Colour the sketched details using fabric paints, crayons or felt-tips. Younger children may prefer to skip step 2 and use colour straight away.

5. Allow the mat to dry, and seal the fabric paint by ironing if necessary, according to the manufacturer's instructions.

6. Dinosaur toys can now be played with on the play mat.

✔ Good practice

Ironing requires close supervision. Younger children will need this task done for them.

Extension Idea

Older children may like to take a more scientific approach to creating their vision of the prehistoric world, based on research. Models can be mounted on painted chipboard or ply. The scenery can be created using materials made for model railway enthusiasts.

Stegosaurus cake

"Bake and decorate a delicious stegosaurus cake. It can be as realistic or as fantastical as you like!**"**

ACTIVITY

S P I C E

Equipment
To make two cakes:
- 110 g butter
- 110 g castor sugar, sieved
- 110 g self-raising flour, sieved
- 2 eggs
- Vanilla essence

- Jam
- Icing and assorted cake decorations
- 2 non-stick 15 cm sandwich tins
- Mixing bowl, wooden spoon, sieve, cooling rack
- Sharp knife, table knife
- Camera (optional)

Instructions

1. Preheat oven to 190°C/375°F/Gas mark 5.
2. Mix the butter and sugar together until light and creamy.
3. Beat in the eggs gradually with a little of the flour.
4. Fold in the remaining flour and vanilla essence.
5. Divide the mixture between the sandwich tins. Bake for 20–25 minutes. Turn out onto a wire rack to cool.
6. Cut the cakes into sections as shown on the diagram below.
7. Assemble the sections as shown, using jam to stick the pieces together.
8. Ice and decorate the cake as desired. Creating spikes of icing along the spine and tail with a fork finishes off the stegosaurus design effectively.
9. Before the cake is sliced and shared, you may like take one or two photos to keep.

For an alternative diabetic sponge recipe visit:
http://sweetnlow.dietaryfoods.co.uk

1. Cut the cake into these sections

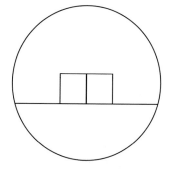

2. Assemble the sections like this, then add icing spikes.

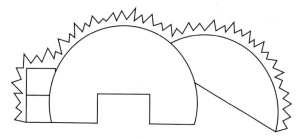

Stegosaurus cake

Extension Idea

Older children can make more complicated decorative cake designs. You can provide party cake books for them to consult, as well allowing them to develop their own unique creations.

ACTIVITY

SPICE

Charades

❝Can you tell a T Rex from a Pterodactyl?❞

Equipment
- Dinosaur pictures
- Index cards
- Glue stick
- Felt-tip pens

Instructions

1. Locate pictures of different types of dinosaurs, and cut them out. Internet printouts are ideal – see the websites section on page 202.

2. Paste the pictures onto index cards, one per card. Write the name of each dinosaur underneath. When dry, stack the cards facedown on the floor. Children should sit in a circle around the cards.

3. Players take turns to enter the circle, choose a card and act out the dinosaur depicted, while the rest of the group tries to guess the name of the dinosaur on the card.

ACTIVITY

SPICE

Dressing-up feet

❝Create your own dressing-up props, and role-play the Jurassic way!❞

Equipment
- Shoe boxes
- Scissors
- Sheets of fun foam
- Masking tape

- Newspaper
- Paint
- Glue stick

Instructions

1. Remove the lids from the shoe boxes. Cut a hole in one end of each box, just large enough for children to slip their feet inside.
2. Scrunch some newspaper into balls. Pack the balls tightly into the front and sides of the boxes, so they will fit the children's feet.
3. Use masking tape to seal the boxes securely. (Ordinary sticky-tape cannot be painted over with water-based paints.)
4. Paint the boxes as desired.
5. Cut sheets of thin coloured foam (from a craft supplier) into triangles, and stick them along the ends of the box lids to make claws. Allow the glue to dry.
6. The shoes are now ready to be worn. You can adjust the size of the feet to fit different children even after the box has been sealed by adding or removing scrunched up paper through the foot hole. It's a good idea to make several pairs of feet so the children can stomp around together!

Scary feet!

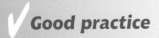

✔ Good practice

Younger children generally need help to cut holes in boxes. Remind children to keep their fingers well clear when pushing scissors through the cardboard.

Websites

Visit:

www.enchantedlearning.com/subjects/dinosaurs for an online dinosaur textbook and printouts

www.rain.org/~philfear/download-a-dinosaur.html for origami patterns suitable for older children

www.nhm.ac.uk for facts and activities from the National History Museum

www.dltk-kids.com/animals/dinosaurs.htm for colouring pages and crafts suitable for younger children

www.dinosaurcartoons.com/index.html for a guide to drawing cartoons

Consultation

It's good practice to consult with children about their play needs and preferences, and this includes asking them about the themes and related planned activities they'd like to participate in.

As well as enabling you to provide play opportunities that children will enjoy, the process of consultation can help children to feel listened to, valued and included. This can lead to increased self-esteem and confidence, and help to encourage the development of feelings of empowerment and ownership.

Consultation can take place during casual conversation as practitioners interact with children. But planned consultation activities can also take place during:

- planning sessions
- evaluations
- reviews.

Methods of consultation

It's important to select a method of consultation that suits the children within your setting. There are many methods to choose from, including:

- *Discussion* You can talk with children individually or in groups about themes and activities, asking them about their preferences and eliciting their own ideas.
- *Questionnaires* These can be written or pictorial, depending on the ages and abilities of the children.
- *Interviews* As an alternative to questionnaires, an 'interviewer' can verbally ask children questions and record their answers. These can be recorded in writing, or via a video camera or tape recorder. The interviewer may be an adult or another child.
- *Suggestion boxes* Children can write and draw their ideas, thoughts and feelings, and put them into a box anonymously. Suggestion video tapes/ audio tapes can also work well, although the element of anonymity is lost.
- *Voting* This may involve a ballot, but it can be as simple as a show of hands, making voting a good, quick way of making final decisions in consultation with your group.

Planning themed activities

Thought-storming is a particularly effective way to consult with children on the planned activities to be included in a forthcoming theme.

Equipment
- Large sheet of paper/whiteboard
- Pens
- Sticky-tack

Instructions

1. Tack a large sheet of paper to the wall, or use a white board. Have the children gather round.

2. Write the title of the theme in the centre of the paper. (The theme may have been decided in a previous vote.)

3. Ask the children to suggest activities linked to the theme. Let them know you need plenty to choose from. At this stage you needn't worry about the feasibility of the ideas, just get them flowing. Write every contribution down, filling the space around your theme title. Make sure you acknowledge/thank all contributors.

4. It's a good idea to ensure the adults in the room have plenty of ideas to chip in between them as this will get the ball rolling and spark off other ideas. You can use the activities included in this book for this purpose.

5. Once a good number of ideas have been generated you can consider them in turn. Some may have to be ruled out because they're inappropriate (often on the grounds of safety or affordability). Explain this to the children. Sometimes you may be able to offer a substitute activity that's reasonably close to the original idea.

6. Talk to the group about the activities that remain on the list, and get a feel for which activities are the most popular. This will inform the programme that you eventually offer. Remember that the overall programme should be varied (see the Introduction on pages v–ix), and that activities should meet the needs of the individual children who will attend the setting during the theme.

Evaluation

Involving children in the evaluation of play sessions reveals what they've enjoyed – this can inform future planning. Try the following visual methods of recording evaluations. Each involves asking children to rank the activities they have participated in, in order of preference.

Bulls-eye evaluation

Equipment
- Large sheet of paper
- Marker pens

Instructions
1. Draw a bulls-eye target on the paper.
2. Explain the meaning of the target rings. (This is shown on the diagram below.)
3. Ask each child to mark a cross on the target to indicate how they felt about a particular planned activity.

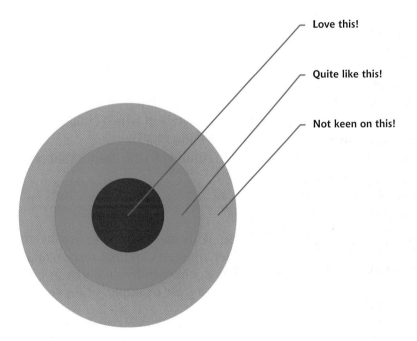

Love this!

Quite like this!

Not keen on this!

Bulls-eye evaluation

Gold, silver and bronze award

Equipment
- Large sheet of paper
- Marker pen
- Gold, silver and bronze stickers

Instructions
1. Write a list of activities on the paper.
2. Equip the children with one gold, one silver and one bronze sticker each.
3. Ask the children to place their stickers next to their favourite activities, using the colours to rank them in first, second and third place.

Corners

Instructions
1. Verbally label each of the four corners of the playground. They should represent 'really liked it', 'liked it', 'didn't like it' and 'really didn't like it'.
2. Call out the titles of the planned activities in which children have participated in turn, e.g. 'The chocolate race!'
3. The children vote with their feet, running to the corner that represents how they felt about that activity.

Extension idea

When working with older children, you can continue to involve them in the next stage of planning. Older children can take responsibility for organising some aspects of activities, either individually or in groups. They may be involved in collecting resources for example, or for setting up an activity on the day.

Encouraging participation

To encourage children to participate in consultation it's a good idea to:
- be motivational in your approach by making the process fun
- communicate the purpose of the consultation to the children, letting them know what they have to say influences future play experiences
- ensure everyone gets their say
- choose methods to suit the children
- ring the changes with regard to the consultation methods used
- acknowledge and accept everyone's contributions
- ensure all contributions are respected.

Additional benefits

Besides putting forward their opinions, consultation can provide children with opportunities to:

- form and explain ideas and opinions
- listen to and respect each other
- discuss and debate
- adapt and negotiate
- plan
- take responsibility
- evaluate
- give feedback
- record information.

Appendix: Example advertising programme

Playtime

Out-of-School Club

Fun for the Half-Term Holidays!

On Monday, 1 June, it's "The Beach" including:
Surf Safari – Make your own cool surfboard and practise your surfing moves!
Sand Sculptures – Make everlasting sandcastles with our special sand dough.
Flapper Fish – Make colourful flapper fish and enter our under-the-water race!

On Tuesday, 2 June, it's "Space" including:
Alien Grass Heads – Make an out-of-this-world alien and see his green hair grow!
Space Race Game – Will your team win a prize in our space race?
Blast Off! – Make and launch your own flying spacecrafts.

On Wednesday, 3 June, it's "Drama" including:
Advertisements – Make your own adverts and show them on "TV".
Improvise! – Put your improvisational skills to the test!
Puppet Theatre – Help to make a puppet theatre and put on a show.

On Thursday, 4 June, it's "The Circus" including:
Juggling Workshop – Learn to juggle, it's so much fun!
Devil Stick Workshop – Learn how to do devil stick tricks.
Big Top – Make a Big Top and perform inside.

On Friday, 5 June, it's our annual "Water Gala" including:
Bulls-eye – Hit the bulls-eye to make a splash in our fun target game.
Relay Races – Can your team save water to win our relay races?
Ice Bowls – Make an elegant ice bowl complete with frozen decorations.

We are open during all the school holidays from 8 a.m. to 6 p.m., Monday to Friday, and each afternoon after school until 6 p.m. during term time. Children from all schools are welcome. To book or for further details, call ******. If your child hasn't attended Playtime before, we recommend you call to arrange a time to visit us prior to booking.

Index

Advertisements, making 36–7
Advertising of activities viii, 208
Age ranges v–vi
Airbrushing 65
Alien grass heads 123–4
Animal tag 182
Animation 116–17
   flip books 119–20
   monkey in a cage 87–8
   thaumatropes 118–19
Art
   collaborative collage 106–7
   fairground 64–5
   moon project 128–9
   rainforest 174–8
Arts Council 12
Astronomy *see* Space

Balancing 168–9
Balloons
   balloon volleyball 17
   juggling 165–6
   pass the buck 16–17
   towel lacrosse 18
Balls
   comet balls 131–2
   make a sports soap 145–6
   making juggling balls 163–4
   whack-a-ball 57–8
Beach 41
   captain's coming 50
   don't rock the boat 43
   flapper fish 42–3
   floating origami boats 52–3
   ice-cream in-a-bag 44
   jelly vessels 51
   resources to support free play 41
   sand sculptures 42
   shark attack 44–5
   surf safari 48–9
   treasure chest 46
   walking the plank 96–7
   wavers and throwers 47–8
   websites 53

Bird on a perch 70–1
Biscuits, coloured star 133
Boats
   don't rock the boat 43–4
   floating origami 52–3
   jelly vessels 51
Boomerang 143–4
Bracelets, friendship 105
Bubbles, giant 24–5
Bulls-eye target game 15

Cake, stegosaurus 198–200
Cameras
   cartridge 5–7
   intangible object collections using 8
   learning to use 2
   photo figures 9–10
   in the picture game 8–9
   special effects 2–3
   using video 10
Captain's coming game 50
Cartoons 116–17
   see also Animation
Catch, comet 132
CBBC 'Press Pack' website 111
Charades, dinosaur 200
Cheat! card game 157–8
Cheerleading 138–9
Chocolate race 98–9
Chopstick challenge 60–1
Chromatography craft 89–90
Circus 161
   balancing act 168–9
   big top 171–2
   devil sticks 166–7
   devil sticks workshop 167–8
   group juggling game 165–6
   juggling balls 163–4
   juggling workshop 164–5
   lasso 162
   performance 170
   resources to support free play 161
   skills workshops 172
   websites 172

Coconut shy 55
Codes 153–4
Collage, collaborative 106–7
Comet balls 131–2
Competition ix
Conga, kangaroo 95–6
Consequences activity 37–8, 108
Consultation with children 203
    benefits for children 207
    encouraging participation in 206
    evaluation of play sessions 204–6
    methods of 203
    planning themed activities 204, 206

Dance workshops 73–4
Dead Ants! 104
Dens, story 92–3
Devil sticks
    making 166–7
    workshop 167–8
Dinosaurs 189
    charades 200
    dressing-up feet 200–1
    egg hunt 190–1
    giant Jurassic game 192–3
    prehistoric habitats 196–8
    resources to support free play 189
    skeleton fossils 193–4
    stegosaurus cake 198–200
    triceratops hoopla 195
    websites 202
Drama 27
    advertisements 36–7
    chocolate race 98–9
    consequences 37–8
    improvise! 29
    masks 185–7
    mime name game 28
    our own programmes 35–6
    in the picture 8–9
    powder and paint 31
    puppet theatre 38–9
    resources to support free play 27
    scriptwriting 32–4
    shark attack 44–5
    websites 40
    white lies 29–30
Drinks
    slush cocktails 183–4
    tropical breakfast smoothies 184
Drumming workshop 104–5

Environmental issues 187

Equipment vii

Fairground 54
    art 64–5
    bottle hoopla 56–7
    bumper car skipping 64
    chopstick challenge 60–1
    coconut shy 55
    hook-a-duck 59–60
    marble challenge 58–9
    resources to support free play 54
    sweet stall 62–3
    websites 65
    whack-a-ball 57–8
Feet, dressing up 200–1
Fence tapestry 86
Film see Photography and film
Film for Youth 12
Fish, flapper 42–3
Flexibility vii
Flip books 119–20
Flip it! 101
Food
    cereal bars 146–7
    coloured star biscuits 133
    fairground fudge 62
    fruit kebab buffet 183
    ice-cream in-a-bag 44
    jelly vessels 51
    slush cocktails 183–4
    stegosaurus cake 198–200
    toffee apples 62–3
    tropical breakfast smoothies 184
Forfeits, blindfold 92
Fossils, skeleton 193–4
Friendship see Teamwork and friendship
Friendship bracelets 105
Friendship wreath 106
Frisbee 142–3
Fudge, fairground 62

Healthy eating ix, 146–7, 183–4
Hoopla
    bottle 56–7
    triceratops 195

Ice bowls 22
Ice sculptures 23
Ice-breaker games 28, 94
    chocolate race 98–9
    improvise! 29
    mime name game 28
    parachute swap 95

in the picture 8–9
shark attack 44–5
stage name game 67–8
white lies 29–30
Ice-cream in-a-bag 44
Inclusion ix
Ink, invisible 153–4
Instructions for activities viii
Instruments, musical 76

Jelly vessels 51
Juggling
group juggling game 165–6
making juggling balls 163–4
workshop 164–5

Kaleidoscope craft, mini 86–7
Kangaroo conga 95–6
Karaoke 77
Kit, designing sports' 144–5

Lacrosse, towel 18
Lasso 162
Light and dark 79
beheaded! 88
blindfold forfeits 92
catching rainbows 89
chromatography craft 89–90
deco 84
fence tapestry 86
follow-the-flashlight 80–1
midday, midnight, twilight 82–3
mini kaleidoscope craft 86–7
mirror challenge 91
monkey in a cage 87–8
resources to support free play 79
shadow puppets 90–1
shadow tag 83–4
story dens 92–3
torchlight explorers 83
torchlight tag 80
websites 93

Magazines
contributions to 111–12
creating a magazine 110–11
Marble challenge 58–9
Masks, making 185–7
Media 109
animation antics 116–17
creating a magazine 110–11
dear editor... 111
flip books 119–20

news magazine programmes 113–15
radio and podcasting 115–16
resources to support free play 109
thaumatropes 118–19
website design 120
websites 121
Mexican wave game 141
Midday, midnight, twilight 82–3
Mime
improvise! 29
name game 28
white lies 29–30
Mirror challenge 91
Monkey in a cage 87–8
Monkey run for tree game 180
Moon art project 128–9
Murder, wink 149
Music 66, 67
bird on a perch 70–1
dance workshop 73–4
drumming workshop 104–5
making 76–8
musical circles 69–70
name that tune 71–2
resources to support free play 66
song writing 68–9
stage name game 67–8
stars in their eyes 75–6
websites 78

Name that tune 71–2
Needles, safety with 127
News magazine programmes 113–15
Noughts and crosses quiz 154–5

Olympic Games, own 135
Olympic spirit 136
Olympic torch 136–8
training 135–6
Origami 52–3

Paints
face 31
spray 26
Parachutes
parachute swap 95
shark attack 44–5
Parrots (art work) 178
Photography and film 1
cartridge cameras 5–7
intangible object collections 8
learning to use a camera 2
photo figures 9–10

photoshoot 75–6
in the picture game 8–9
pinhole viewer 4–5
resources to support free play 1
roll the credits 11–12
special effects 2–3
sun photo art 7
using a video camera 10
websites 13
Pinhole viewer 4–5
Planetarium, mini 126–7
Podcasts 115
Pom-poms 138–9
Problem-solving see Puzzles
Programmes, making own 35–6, 113–15
Puppet theatre 38–9
Puppets, shadow 90–1
Puzzles 148, 149
cheat! 157–8
get knotted! 150–1
guess who? 156–7
invisible ink 153–4
noughts and crosses quiz 154–5
playground word search 152
puzzle partners 151
resources to support free play 148
sitting, standing, bending, crouching
159–60
snaky, snaky 155–6
websites 160
wink murder 149

Radio 115–16
Rainbows, catching 89
Rainforest 173
animal tag 182
art 174–8
environmental issues 187
making masks 185–7
monkey run for tree 180
resources to support free play 173
snakes alive! 181
tiger tails game 179–80
tropical treats 183–4
websites 188
Recipes see Food
Relay races, with water 20–1
Resources vii
Risk assessment viii–ix
Rockets 124–6, 129–31
Rosettes 139–41

Sand sculptures 42

Sawdust, safety with 124
Scriptwriting 32–4
Shadow puppets 90–1
Shadow tag 83–4
Shark attack 44–5
Skipping
bumper car 64
challenge with water 19
Snakes
snakes alive! 181
snaky, snaky 155
spiral 176–7
Song writing 68–9
Space 122
alien grass heads 123–4
blastoff! 129–31
coloured star biscuits 133
comet catch 131–2
moon surface 128–9
resources to support free play 122
space race game 124–6
space suits 127
stargazer scopes 126
websites 134
SPICE vi–vii
Sport 135
boomerang 143–4
cheerleading 138–9
Frisbee 142–3
healthy eating 146–7, 183–4
kit design 144–5
make a sports soap 145–6
Mexican wave game 141
Olympic torch 136–8
own Olympic Games 135–6
resources to support free play 135
rosettes 139–41
websites 147
Stage name game 67–8
Star biscuits, coloured 133
Sticky buds 99–100
Sun-Print paper 7
Surfboards and surfing 48–9

Tag
animal 182
shadow 83–4
torchlight 80
Target games 196
bottle hoopla 56–7
bulls-eye 15
triceratops hoopla 195
Teamwork and Friendship 94

chocolate race 98–9
collaborative collage 106–7
consequences 37–8, 108
dead ants! 104
drumming workshop 104–5
flip it! 101
friendship bracelets 105
friendship wreath 106
kangaroo conga 95–6
parachute swap 95
puzzle partners 151
relay races 20–1
resources to support free play 94
space race game 124–5
sticky buds 99–100
team identity 101–2
walking the plank 96–7
wavers and throwers 47–8
websites 108
Thaumatropes 118–19
Tiger tails game 179–80
Toffee apples 62–3
Torches
follow-the-flashlight 80–1
mirror challenge 91
torchlight explorers 83
torchlight tag 80
Towel lacrosse 18
Treasure chest 46

Video
adding credits 11–12
making advertisements 36
making programmes 35–6, 113–15
using a video camera 10
Volleyball, balloon 17

Water 14
balloon volleyball 17
bulls-eye 15
giant bubbles 24–5
ice bowls 22
ice sculptures 23
pass the buck 16–17
relays 20–1
resources to support free play 14
skipping challenge 19
spray paint 26
towel lacrosse 18
under and over game 16
websites 26
Website design 120
Websites ix
Wink murder 149
Word search, playground 152
Wreath, friendship 106